FAILURE IS NEVER FINAL

How To Bounce Back BIG From Any Defeat

Vic Johnson & Champions
From Around The World

Laurenzana Press

Copyright © 2016 Laurenzana Press
All Rights Reserved

This publication may not be reproduced, stored in a retrieval system, or transmitted in whole or in part, in any form or by any means, electronic, mechanical, photocopying, recording, or otherwise—with the exception of a reviewer who may quote brief passages in a review to be printed in a newspaper or magazine—without prior written permission from the Publisher.

Published by:
Laurenzana Press
PO Box 1220
Melrose, FL 32666 USA

www.LaurenzanaPress.com

ISBN-13: 978-1-937918-88-0

Printed in the United States of America

Book interior design by Jean Boles
jean.bolesbooks@gmail.com

CONTRIBUTING AUTHORS

Vic Johnson

Joan Warren

Paula Hayashi, MD

Gregory Corradino, MD MBA

John Bell

Peggy McIntire

Dr. Jill Fjelstul

Darrin O. Thomas

Dean Mannheimer

Jeff Spedding

Jennifer Barna

Vanessa Wray

Albina Gabellini

Thomas Hutcherson

Joan Junker

Steve Highsmith

Doug Evans

Joel Johnson

TABLE OF CONTENTS

INTRODUCTION: A New Definition Of Failure 7
   by Vic Johnson

CHAPTER ONE: Confronting the Bull 15
   by Joan Warren

CHAPTER TWO: The Dark Night of My Soul 23
   by Paula Hayashi MD

CHAPTER THREE: We Regret to Inform You 33
   by Gregory Corradino, MD MBA

CHAPTER FOUR: Faith Rises from the Ashes 41
   by John Bell

CHAPTER FIVE: Overflow 49
   by Peggy McIntire

CHAPTER SIX: Mulligans 57
   by Dr. Jill Fjelstul

CHAPTER SEVEN: The Wisdom of Failure 65
   by Darrin O. Thomas

CHAPTER EIGHT: I Didn't Know I Didn't Know 73
   by Dean Mannheimer

CHAPTER NINE: The Stranger Named Bill 81
   by Jeff Spedding

CHAPTER TEN: Finding Forgiveness and Gratitude in the Depths of My Despair Turned My Life Around 89
   by Jennifer Barna

CHAPTER ELEVEN: Rare Hidden Diamonds in Wounded Butterfly Cocoons 97
   by Vanessa Wray

CHAPTER TWELVE: Passion, Perseverance, Resilience: Alex Zanardi, a Champion 105
   by Albina Gabellini

CHAPTER THIRTEEN: The Courage to Continue................................. 115
   by Thomas Robert Hutcherson

CHAPTER FOURTEEN: Greek Olympic Athlete Trains Running Barefoot on Rocks to Feed His Country 123
   by Joan Junker

CHAPTER FIFTEEN: A Radical Faith Does Radical Things................. 131
   by Steve Highsmith

CHAPTER SIXTEEN: I Brought the Monster to Its Knees.................... 139
   by Doug Evans

CHAPTER SEVENTEEN: The Cinderella Men.. 147
   by Joel Johnson

CHAPTER EIGHTEEN: What to Do Now.. 155
   by Vic Johnson

ABOUT VIC JOHNSON 161

BOOKS BY VIC JOHNSON.. 163

INTRODUCTION

A New Definition Of Failure
by Vic Johnson

In 1966 Maxcy Filer took the California Bar exam for the first time at the age of 36 and failed. He took it again and failed once more. He took it again and again and again, and each time he failed. He took it in Los Angeles, San Diego, Riverside, San Francisco and anywhere else it was offered. He took it when his children were still living at home and he took it with each of his sons when they had earned their own law degrees. He took it after he started working as a law clerk in the law offices of his sons, and he kept taking it even as he reached an age when most people are thinking of retirement. He failed each time.

After twenty-five years, $50,000 in exam fees and review courses, and 144 days of his life spent in testing rooms, Maxcy Filer took the bar exam for the 48th time and passed. He was 61 years old. Maxcy never saw each failure as the end of his dream. The failures were merely steps toward his dream.

Failure. The very word strikes fear in many of us. The idea that we might attempt to achieve something that we want at a deep level—to put our deepest desires on the line—and fall short, is downright scary. And when we do make ourselves vulnerable, whether it's in a job interview or submitting that latest manuscript to a publisher, we feel like our fate is in someone else's hands.

To many people, a failed attempt at something is evidence. They consider it *evidence* that their negative talk and self-doubts were right all along. They use failures as excuses to point out the worst of their own flaws or, worse yet, they don't do anything about them because they're too discouraged to continue on.

But here's a secret about failure they won't tell you.

When you fail—when you fall flat on your face because you reached too high—that means you are at least on the path to something new. Failure is messy. It's loud. It's uncomfortable. Failure is what many people fear so much that they don't even take action.

But what's more peaceful than failure? What's more quiet than being rejected?

Simple: doing absolutely nothing at all.

You see, it's not the failures that define us—it's the moments of breakthrough. And you don't get to moments of breakthrough by sitting around and hoping that one day you'll start taking action. You don't get to moments of breakthrough by accepting failure at face value, believing your self-doubts to be accurate and quitting altogether.

We have this concept of failure that we use to define our fears. We think that if we embarrass ourselves by trying something new and tanking in front of others, we'll look like a "loser," or, yes, a "failure."

The truth is, when you attempt something that causes you fear, most of the time, other people *admire* you for it on a deeper level.

Because they wish *they* were as impervious to failure as you are.

Failure is a matter of perspective, and it's only when you accept failure's finality that it becomes real. After all, there are countless examples of people in the past who have objectively "failed" but refused to accept the finality of that failure.

Mary Kay Ash

The story of Mary Kay Ash is a perfect example of persevering in the face of constant obstacles while staying flexible.

While her husband served in the military during World War II, Mary Kay Ash earned extra money by selling books door to door. Soon after her husband's return in 1945, they divorced—in a time when divorce was far less common than it is today. That was a difficult failure, to be sure, but Ash kept chugging along to earn money, going to work for Stanley Home Products. There, she helped train an employee (a man), who eventually earned a promotion she had coveted.

Ash decided to retire from that business, but not to quit working. Although she originally intended to write a book for women in business, the research that went into the book eventually coalesced into a business plan. She planned to start that new company with her new husband, but a month before the launch, he unexpectedly died of a heart attack.

At that point, one can imagine feeling tempted to quit. Who wouldn't? The grief over losing a new husband, the frustration of working so hard in business only to see every attempt at success thwarted... it's a lot for anyone to handle.

But Mary Kay Ash was no ordinary woman. She continued with the business plan, accepted a $5,000 investment from her son, and started the business she'd always dreamed of.

She started Mary Kay Cosmetics.

That company is now worth billions in revenue every year and has helped launch the careers of many other businesswomen who had the same dreams as Mary Kay Ash. What lessons can we glean from her story?

For starters, Mary Kay Ash never quit. She adjusted her plans, to be sure, but she never adjusted her overall vision of helping people in business. She abandoned the book, yes, but she turned that idea into a concrete company that would help people through action, not words. She accomplished all of her goals and then some because she was flexible enough to see multiple paths to the top, and she never saw finality in the failure she experienced.

Stephen King
It's tempting to think of Stephen King as the "master of horror" and to imagine that he has never been anything else. But for a long time, he was a failed writer. In fact, he was a failed writer for years—certainly a long enough time that most people would bow out of the profession altogether, assuming that they didn't have what it takes to get published.

Stephen King demonstrated a high tolerance to failure when he put up a nail in the wall. This nail would hold all of his rejections: every time he received a rejection slip, he'd post it through the nail on the wall.

How many of us give up after five rejections? Ten rejections? Twenty? A hundred?

The truth is, most of us would have given up well before Stephen King did.

In fact, Stephen King kept writing even after the nail became so full of rejections that it couldn't hold any more.

Did he stop writing? Did he "take the hint"? He easily could have. Instead, he replaced the nail with a spike and kept on writing.

Eventually, the rejections grew a little bit warmer. Editors would reply with revisions that he could make, little changes to the text that would change his writing. Stephen King, rather than ever giving up, took the warmer rejections as signs that he was making progress. He made the changes and eventually, he sold his first stories.

These days, Stephen King doesn't have to worry so much about rejections.

The lesson here: most of us would consider such an overwhelming amount of failure an obvious sign from the world that you were not "cut out" for the career you sought. Anyone with any degree of prudence or reason would simply go on with their day job and abandon their loftier dreams. But Stephen King, today known as a prolific and successful author, was not *born* that way. He made himself that way by channeling lessons learned from failure and rejection into continuous improvement.

The world of publishing is full of similar scenarios. The mega, best-selling series *Chicken Soup for The Soul* was rejected by the first 144 publishers to which it was pitched. But Jack Canfield and Mark Victor Hansen never totally lost their belief in the project and have gone on to sell over 500 million copies.

Whenever you think about how many rejections you've faced, visualize that nail on the wall full of Stephen King's rejections and ask yourself if you've really put your skills to the test yet.

James Dyson
We're all familiar with Thomas Edison's approach to the light bulb. He reportedly went through hundreds of variations in his attempt to discover how to light the world. When asked about his failures, Edison is commonly believed to have said that he didn't fail—he only discovered ways that didn't work.

We all know the Edison story, but how many of us know the James Dyson story?

James Dyson is the pioneer of the DC bagless vacuum—an invention that, like the light bulb, we take for granted today. We never consider just how much sweat and tears went into the product; we simply enjoy the fruits of an inventor's labor.

No one labored harder than Dyson. He reportedly went through over 5,000 variations of the bagless vacuum cleaner before he could consider it "perfected." That's not only a lot of work, but a lot of upfront investing: you don't build that many prototypes without funding some of it yourself. To struggle that hard and to invest that much time and energy into one product might seem strange to some—maybe even doomed to failure.

Dyson certainly didn't see it that way himself. Though none of the leading names in the vacuum industry wanted his product, he still believed in it. After the point in which most people would assume they had failed, Dyson decided to double down: he would start his own company and manufacture the bagless vacuum cleaner *himself*.

Today, Dyson is one of the top names in vacuum cleaners with a net worth estimated to be billions of dollars. Some people have called him the world's first billionaire inventor. But he certainly would be none of those things if he had a different kind of reaction to failure—the kind of reaction that *most* people have to failure.

What You'll Get Out of This Book
If you currently let your fear of failure dictate your actions, we have some work to do before you develop the perseverance of a James Dyson.

But that doesn't mean that greatness is outside of your grasp. It's available to anyone who is willing to go through failures and keep going strong.

In this book, you'll find countless examples, lessons, and insights into what it means to feel like you've failed and come out stronger on the other side. You'll read insights from physicians, a golf professional turned college professor, entrepreneurs, a sales executive—and many more.

As the world judges them, they are successful. They've achieved notoriety and prosperity in their chosen fields. However, you might be surprised to learn just how much failure they had to endure on their way to the top.

In other chapters, some of our co-authors will share the story of failures who inspired them by their refusal to accept failure as finality.

And that's what this book is about. Not about fearing failure, but about recognizing the role of failure in your personal development. It will show you that what you *believe* to be failures are often just opportunities in disguise—or, at the very least, a form of feedback that can help you on your journey and hone your focus so you're even stronger tomorrow.

Read this book with an open mind and try to absorb the lessons. Put yourself in the shoes of the authors. Really imagine what it might have been like if you were in their position—how you might have thought negative things about yourself, how you might have given up. And when you find yourself with new insights into what failure is, try applying those same insights into *your* life.

The most important lesson: failure is not permanent unless you make it that way. Failure is simply an event that transpires. It has no bearing on your future prosperity or success. It has no bearing on your past. The only relevance failure has is what you choose to give it. The only emotional resonance failure can have is what *you choose* to interpret.

You are not a failure unless you give up, "pack up your tent," and walk away from the game. So long as you remain at the table, there's always a chance for success.

Bottom line? Failure is never final. It wasn't for Mary Kay Ash, Stephen King, or James Dyson—and it isn't for you, either.

- **Vic Johnson**

CHAPTER ONE

Confronting the Bull
by Joan Warren

"Expect challenges and accept change to live in the now with gratitude."

~ Joan Marilyn Warren

I was born into a strict, religious family. At the age of four, I had an eye operation. Unfortunately, I lost the ability to smell when my sight was saved. This disability has affected me throughout my life; an invisible disability is an unrecognized challenge.

As a young child, I intensely disliked an often-played party game that involved identifying an object by smell while blindfolded. It didn't take long for the other kids to discover my handicap and make fun of me. I felt terribly upset! I soon retreated from all group activity. My parents ignored my feelings of extreme discomfort, so I suffered in silent embarrassment.

I was only six when my first music teacher rapped my knuckles with a ruler whenever I made a mistake. It stung so much that I deliberately failed my grade one piano exam, and I was happy my lessons ended. However, my parents believed the examiner who said that I had no musical ability.

When I was thirteen, I heard the organ at church, and I had a sudden longing to learn to play such beautiful music. The organist told me she would teach me to play if I first got my grade eight piano degree from the Royal Conservatory of Music. When I asked my parents for piano lessons, they told me it would be a waste of money. Using my babysitting earnings, I hired a piano teacher. My love of practicing moved me through the grades with phenomenal speed. My music became a haven of joy where I could fly away to hide whenever I felt ignored or hurt.

At fourteen, I met a church member who was twelve years older than me, and I was allowed to date him. I enjoyed this time of growing because we always went in couples to concerts, ballets, and operas. I never dated anyone else.

When I entered marriage, at age twenty, my fairytale situation changed. I became confused and unhappy because, in the eyes of my husband, I suddenly couldn't do anything right. The three C's of criticizing, condemning, and complaining filled my marriage. I had left my parents' home and moved directly into my husband's newly built, unfinished house only to discover that I was expected to keep house and have children with no aspirations for a career. Each day I received a job list, and at the end of the day, my perfectionist husband would examine my work. He always found something that I had done wrong. Six months later, feeling dejected, I left my husband. My father commanded me to return, saying that you marry for better or worse and telling me to "Love more, and everything will be all right."

Endeavoring to make my relationship successful, I ignored my needs. I was afraid to tell anyone what was happening. I was expected to accept my husband's judgments, obey him, and quickly correct my mistakes. I was told this would make me happy. Needless to say, it didn't work. Instead, I cried a lot and lost confidence in myself.

One day, while preparing dinner for guests, I made a floral arrangement with dramatic, yellow wildflowers. I was proud of how bright and beautiful the table looked. Fortunately, our guests arrived before my husband returned from work and made me aware that I had chosen unwisely. They light-heartedly teased me as we aired out the house of the unpleasant smell. Unknowingly, I had chosen skunk cabbage flowers, unaware that they smelled disgusting.

Later, I received the full blast of my husband's exasperation. How could I possibly not know that the flowers reeked like a skunk? All I needed to do was "believe" that I could smell, and I would know the difference between good and bad odors. My explanation about the eye operation at the age of four fell on deaf ears and my feelings of being ignored and scorned intensified.

Even though his comments were hurtful, the incident didn't end there. He made me the subject of his ridicule by repeating the story of the "skunk in the house" many times over. I pleaded with him to stop, but he refused. It was then I realized that I could change myself, but not someone else.

From that day on, I decided to ignore his continuous criticisms and hurtful remarks. I smothered the frustration and hurt. I was naïve in that I didn't know that this action would destroy my ability to feel both negative and positive emotions, or that it would lead to chronic depression.

Eight years into our marriage, we adopted a seven-month-old baby girl. Two years later, I became pregnant, and while giving birth to our daughter, I had a near-death experience. Miraculously, an emergency caesarean section saved both our lives. At this time, I had a spiritual vision, and protecting my little ones became my primary concern.

Three years after the birth of our daughter, we moved to Peterborough, Ontario to work on a buffalo ranch. One day, a bull attempted to escape across the five-foot-wide creek that ran through the property. I stood on the opposite side, and, staring at the animal, I used a quiet, monotone voice to instruct him to turn around and go back into the enclosure. He snorted and pawed the ground, but I refused to move even though I knew that he planned to charge. Finally, this majestic animal shook his head, turned around, and retreated to the fenced area where I had ordered him to go.

This incident helped me claim freedom from the "what will happen, if…" question. What would my parents, sisters, or others think? I was suddenly no longer afraid of what others thought about what I chose to do. I wanted respect. By demanding this, I created havoc, especially when I would state emphatically, "I disagree." My husband found this unacceptable.

I loved working on the farm; my husband hated it. By the time a year had passed, my husband had created a situation that made it impossible for me to continue working on the farm. We purchased a home (with my parents, to assist in the financial challenges). I felt terrible, and I gained an excessive amount of weight as I struggled to make ends meet.

I began to meditate frequently. The words "I can do it" remained my motto, but I had changed, and the feeling that we needed to separate became intense. I started to work selling office equipment to increase our income. Shortly after, my husband joined the same firm.

Our twenty-fifth wedding anniversary was approaching when my boss presented me with a gift certificate to a restaurant, suggesting that we celebrate. I purchased a new dress for the occasion and was ready to go when my husband ordered me to change my clothes, stating that he would not go unless I did. After the tension-filled evening was over, I cried for hours. When I arrived, red-eyed, at work the next day, the boss's wife asked me what had happened.

That same day, my boss asked me to go with him on a three-day business trip. During the journey, he asked me to clarify why I was staying in what he believed was an abusive marriage. He made it clear that there are two kinds of abuse, physical and emotional. I explained that the threat of financial insecurity was hanging over my head. Suggesting that my confidence was being affected, he informed me that he had been thinking of giving me a promotion to sales manager, but was concerned about the effect it would have on my working relationship with my husband. I was surprised and apprehensive because I knew the promotion would have a disastrous impact on my marriage.

When I returned from the trip, a member of the staff told me that my husband believed I was having an affair with my boss and that he had joined the firm to keep an eye on me. This happened in the spring of 1980. I moved from Ontario to British Columbia with my children four months later.

I felt guilty for having failed my marriage. I believed that I had to remain separated and finish raising my kids without assistance from any other source. I was convinced that I was doing the right thing for all of us. At that point, I asked for help and received, for a short time, excellent counseling from the director of the Single Parents Association in Victoria, BC.

It was at this time I realized that I had to find my real self. To me, that meant I needed to become financially secure and remain independent, away from the constant negativity my husband delivered on a regular basis. I needed to welcome and accept the changes in my life and conquer fear—specifically, the fear of bankruptcy.

The counselor recommended self-help books, including financial management guides, for me to study. While studying, I discovered that guilt and fear are like stop signs. When I felt guilty, I could not act. If I feared the results of an action, I would not act.

Repeating a mantra several times a day helped. The words that helped me most were, "Keep going and don't look back. Failure is not forever. It is a stepping-stone." I also discovered a quote by C.S. Lewis that I found encouraging. "Failures are finger posts on the road to achievement."

A couple of years later, I met a potential client who changed my life when he asked me to speak to his association group at their next meeting, stating that he was impressed with my presentation. He trusted me, and because of this, I gained new friendships, business, and a happy, intimate relationship.

In 2000, I was diagnosed with Merkel cell carcinoma, a rare and aggressive skin cancer. However, I didn't allow fear to stop me. Blinded by tears, I walked over to where my second husband was waiting, thinking, "I can't die—my husband needs me." Even though I felt concerned, I knew I was going to fight and win.

During my cancer treatment, a counselor from the BC Cancer Agency suggested that I consider writing as an outlet to help free myself from the fear of cancer. When I responded that I couldn't, she asked why not, and I explained that a high school English teacher had told me never to think about a career in writing and threatened to fail me in English.

Her response jarred me. "This is now. Let go of what the past story is telling you and move forward with the now."

As I considered her words, I came to see that the things my English teacher had said were in conflict with other memories, memories that indicated that I could indeed write. I realized that there was a pattern in my life dictated by the beliefs that I had accepted about myself. I decided to make another change and find my voice.

I started by writing poetry. Then I penned a novel, which I shelved because I had accomplished my goal of self-expression and was cancer-free. My granddaughter and I are now publishing the novel as an e-book on Amazon/Kindle, and I plan to create a website to share my poetry and other ideas. As I no longer fear failure, I am happy and grateful for my successes.

If you want to ascend a mountain, you need to train and exercise to develop the physical strength and practical knowledge required to make the climb. Failure never guarantees another failure, unless you do not make any changes.

Question your beliefs. I did. Either you will confirm them as right for you, or you will discover that a change in "belief" will make you happier. Challenges—some mundane, others huge—face us every day. As you make the choices, trust yourself. Ask for help to get the guidance you need and conquer the fears that haunt you. Refuse to give up, no matter how long it takes to reach your goal.

The words "happiness" and "successes" are followed by question marks because only you can know what will make you happy, and success means something different to everyone. It is your life, and you can choose to live with joy. I do, so I know you can also.

ABOUT THE AUTHOR

Joan Warren lives with her family in Victoria, British Columbia and is writing poetry and articles to share her life experiences. She is an avid reader. She retired in 1995 from sales and traveled with her husband to many different countries. Joan's career was varied—secretarial, sales, and music. She believes it is never too late to try something new and for the past year has been co-authoring with her granddaughter, who lives in Sweden.

You may contact her at **joanwarrenbc@gmail.com** or **www.joinjoan.ca.**

CHAPTER TWO

The Dark Night of My Soul
by Paula Hayashi MD

*"If your heart is in your dream
No request is too extreme
When you wish upon a star
Like dreamers do."*

**~ Leigh Harline and Ned Washington,
Walt Disney's 1940 adaptation of** *Pinocchio*

Have you ever felt like your life was a series of setbacks? That each step took you further away from your goals instead of helping you move forward?

Well, I've gone through times when everything felt like that.

Early in my years at med school, I began to see the presence of God in our lives. I started to recognize an intriguing harmony and order evident simply in how the body works, and this observation acted as proof that a higher power exists behind that harmony.

At the same time that I became aware of this, two events made me contemplate the meaning of life. My close friend committed suicide and my fiancée died of cancer. These significant experiences made me stop and think.

I was sexually abused, and as a result I had to take a cocktail of AIDS medications and antibiotics to prevent a potential infection. All my tutors in residency told me that I would experience several side effects, and I was warned that the medications could really affect my work and shifts. That's when I saw how God works: *I had no side effects at all.* It was like drinking pure water! I actually wondered if I had been given placebo medications! The blood tests came out normal. I started to think there must be a God after all!

By the second year of residency, my 16-year-old cousin, who was like a little brother to me, died in a car accident. This made me ask the question: What are God's intentions for us? I started to look for that God I had first found in my studies.

At that point, I fell in love. We worked several shifts in residency together. We started dating, and it seemed like everything was going well. But when the residency finished, he went back to his home town and wasn't able to commit to the relationship. I suffered a lot at that time. I didn't have much knowledge about relationships, which I have now. I was frustrated, brokenhearted, and I met the first stages of depression right then.

Subconsciously, I decided that passion was just not good for me.

Then a friend of mine insisted on introducing me to her friend. And just because he was nice to me and made me laugh, I started dating him. Unfortunately, I didn't feel any physical attraction; I did not fall in love. I was just using the relationship to cope with the depression because I really was still in love with that other guy, the one who disappeared at the end of his residency.

I ended up marrying the man who was really the opposite of who I am! Our likes and friends were so completely different that I felt like this ugly duck. Remember the story of a swan growing up in a family of ducks? I felt like I was not a nice person since I couldn't fit in with his friends. I felt bad and guilty.

At the time, I went to psychotherapy sessions. One time, as we were discussing these feelings I had of not fitting in, my psychotherapist said, "Remember the ugly duck turned out to be a swan!" I didn't realize it at the time, but she was delivering a message from God to me. I held onto her words of encouragement, but I was not yet aware of the big picture.

It was around this time that my marriage went through a crisis. I was working really hard then, making 80 percent of our total household income, and I was really, really tired. As happens to people who are overworked, diseases started to come into my life.

First, I herniated a disc in my lower spine, which left me bedridden for several days. I couldn't even use the toilet by myself! The tremendous pain and the feeling of powerlessness crippled me. I didn't understand it back then, but God was trying to say something to me. I felt He was trying to tell me to *stop*, but it would take me years to realize what I needed to *stop doing*. Heavy painkillers did not relieve the intense back pain; I only found relief from acupuncture sessions—nothing else! That's when I started to study more. I wanted to know why acupuncture works better than heavy medications. This caused me to see the healing process from a very different perspective.

A few years later, in the middle of a crisis in my marriage, I noticed a strange rash on my skin that appeared out of the blue. It scared me a great deal because I knew it could be a serious disease. Desperate, I called my friend, a very competent hematologist that knew about my personal life. She told me, "You know, this could be something serious, and it could be nothing—some nonspecific process." With her beautiful green eyes, black hair, and lovely voice, she said, "But there's the other side of the coin, you know.... You must consider your emotional situation. You really need to change your life. If you don't do this now, you may hurt yourself even more later. So please, dear, do something."

At the time, I felt like my husband (now my ex-husband) was going in one direction and I was going in another, completely different, direction. I wanted to feel loved and protected, and this man was not able to give me what I needed. I cried often, sometimes many times a day. I asked myself what was I doing with my life. I just couldn't find meaning in working so hard, in this relationship, and in dealing with the many diseases—it was too much. I felt aware that all of these problems could be another message from God. I knew I had to do something, but still, I didn't have the courage to act.

A year after that, I was still struggling. I went for a mammogram screening test and the results showed microcalcifications. As a result, I had a mammotomy—the doctor had to remove the microcalcifications for analysis. That's when I got really, really scared. My ex was more worried about how much he had to pay for this procedure than the competence of the professional doing it—or my life. Thank God, it was nothing. But all of this made me wonder: What is God trying to say to me?

I researched and tested alternative healing methods, treatments, and spirituality. I started to ask myself what the purpose of my life was, but I just couldn't find a satisfying answer.

One day I was in an alternative medicine workshop when a doctor (whom I had never met before) initiated small conversation with me. As we were speaking, she suddenly said, "I need to deliver a message to you." She then said, "You know... your life will change. You will have some shifts in your life, and many people that are in your life right now will disappear."

I was in shock; I couldn't say a word. She continued, saying, "Your husband, some of your relatives, and you, will all really change."

I was not ready for that. I went to a washroom and cried. When would this happen? How will I live then? I was so afraid to face this moment—so afraid that I kept going.

I was just surviving— that is, until the movie *The Secret* came out. It was like fresh air! It filled me with hope that something could change for the better.

I started to search for the mentors in *The Secret* and decided to go for a yearlong coaching program with one of them. My ex couldn't agree with that. He thought it was too expensive, especially since I was only making a low salary at that time (because I had decided not to work that hard any longer). Now, I thank God so much for that opportunity. I started to shift my mindset; I felt that at last I could change.

Small changes started to manifest, and at first I thought my marriage could improve.

But, in fact, God sent me His two last messages. In December of 2008, my ex started to humiliate me in front of his friends, and after a while, in front of my own family. This disrespect really broke my heart. I thought I would never recover from that. It was not an issue of forgiving him because I did indeed forgive him. It was an issue of needing to heal my heart. Deep inside, I felt it was the end.

I talked to God, saying, "I understand your message now in the deepest part of my soul." And the decision came naturally—it was time to separate. I thought, "Let me give him a chance to be happy. This will enable me a chance to be happy as well." It was a hard decision to make after nine years of marriage, not knowing how I would live without him. But I'd hit rock bottom; divorce was the only choice.

One month after all the papers were done, I was sitting on my bed when a sincere prayer grew in my heart.

"God, please, please help me, because I don't know what else to do with my life." I was not satisfied with my profession, I had a failed marriage, and I was feeling like there was something missing, but I could not figure out what that was. I was about to give up.

Two weeks after that moment, I was referred by my psychotherapist to a workshop about femininity.

I was so tired of suffering. I thought that would be the last thing I would do. However, I went to the workshop. It was my only hope at the time.

The person conducting the workshop referred me to this master for a consultation. I didn't know much about this master then; I just went.

And then I had my meeting with God!

It was like the hand of God in my life, leading me off the road of sufferings and onto a road of bliss.

I just knew I could trust him. Everything he said made so much sense! He said I was supposed to be a spiritual healer and that I was not fulfilling my life's purpose, which was why I felt such deep dissatisfaction.

After that workshop, I went on several spiritual retreats. I learned different eastern healing techniques, such as yoga and meditation, which helped me so very much. I engaged in multiple healing sessions and started to discover and heal my inner woman. I learned the truth about relationships. My lifestyle changed significantly.

I now know the purpose of my life. I realize that, in fact, I had always known of it, ever since I was a little girl. When I was six years old and my cousin was seven years old, he tripped and fell, hurting his knee. I was so happy taking care of his knee! I was destined to be a healer.

After 20 years of research and testing different healing techniques in my own life, I now help people in many different ways. I teach yoga classes, spiritual healing lectures, and feminine knowledge classes. I conduct Circle Healing Prayer meditations, helping hundreds of people heal their bodies and souls. It all fills my heart with such a great feeling of fulfillment.

I'm now creating a series of transformational audios, combining science and technology with ancient knowledge; I want these audios to help people live happier lives and to realize their dreams.

God speaks to us in many ways and through a wide variety of situations and people. Each interaction with a person is simply God speaking to us.

I have wonderful things happening in my life these days, but there are always things to work on. Now I observe people and situations in my life in order to better understand what God is trying to communicate.

I hope my story will help you overcome your own challenges in life and empower you to find your true and best life. I know if I can do it, you can, too!

God is always showing us whether we are on the right track and if we are fulfilling our life's purpose. He will continue sending His messages until we listen to them.

The reality is that the purpose of your life is just one: to be happy!

Ask yourself: Am I happy?

What would make me happy?

What were my dreams when I was a little girl or boy?

What did I enjoy doing?

Be thankful to God for what you have right now—the good and the bad. This is the most important thing! All experiences, good and bad, exist for your growth.

Let go of your past. It does not serve you any longer. Forgive everybody. Most of all, forgive yourself.

And then from the depths of your heart, start imagining your dream life. Start living this secret life in your heart and mind, as if it has already come true. How great you feel! How happy you are! How wealthy and healthy you are in this new life. You have it already in your mind and heart; it's just a matter of time before your dreams come true.

Make the decision to do it!

I wish you the best and happiest life!

ABOUT THE AUTHOR

Paula Hayashi MD is a medical doctor specializing in Gynecology/Obstetrics, Diagnostic Imaging, and Chinese Medicine.

She lived through a close friend´s suicide and witnessed her fiancés death from cancer during her medical school years. She ended her nine-year failing marriage six years ago, faced with diseases and other difficult situations, and a growing dissatisfaction in her professional life. It seemed like life was over...

She was about to give up, when after a sincere prayer, an encounter with a divine master from the eastern world led to the fulfilment of her life´s purpose.

Currently she conducts Circle Healing Prayer Meditations, lectures and counselling sessions on spiritual healing, life´s purpose, harmonious relationships, yoga and feminine knowledge. She is now building her online business. "I finally achieved inner peace, health and love!"

www.LightSourceScience.com

Facebook: Po Tara Tora

https://www.facebook.com/Circle-Healing-Prayer-164597413877754/

CHAPTER THREE

We Regret to Inform You
by Gregory Corradino, MD MBA

"A failure is a lesson, sometimes harsh, but a lesson nevertheless."
~ Unknown

I'm a neurosurgeon who has been in practice for 26 years. It is a demanding profession, given the difficulties of the problems we often face. There are sometimes very sick patients with incurable problems whom I see and treat. Often, I take care of people with physically, intellectually, and emotionally draining difficulties; I would not have been able to succeed had I not learned how to face up to tough situations and meet them head on throughout my career. People think it was a steady rise to get here, but there have been many bumps and detours along the way.

Just getting into medical school was the first challenge I faced. I grew up in a working class neighborhood in southern New Jersey. It was all my parents could do to raise six children on my dad's salary. I worked hard in high school and set my sights on going to Notre Dame University. However, my family simply didn't have the money to send me there. My father was transferred to a job in Washington, DC and my family moved to Virginia just as I graduated high school. With no other prospects and no real advice about a career, I started college at Northern Virginia Community College. I transferred after my first year to George Mason University near our home and decided to major in biology.

Starting in my sophomore year, I began to think about what I would do when I finished school and began to consider medicine as a career. I took the required classes and asked my professors for their advice and counsel. I then took the medical school admission test (the MCAT) and did well.

Back then (late 1970s), there was no Internet or Google to easily research medical schools. Where did I have the best chance of being accepted? How much would the school cost? What kind of grades were required? It was off to the school library to sift through medical school catalogs and write away for applications. Once the application was in hand, it had to be handled with care and typed out by hand on a typewriter. There was no online application process, and when using a typewriter there is no such thing as backspace if you make a typo. Oh, we had "white-out," but too much of that and the paper looked like a rodent had been nibbling at the pages. Once I had my four applications ready, along with my transcripts and essay on "Why I Want to Be a Doctor," it was off to the post office. The application process itself had taken weeks. Now all I could do was wait (nervously) for the acceptance letters.

Which never came.

Instead, I received a stream of letters that began "Dear Mr. Corradino: We regret to inform you…" There was no "nice try" or "you almost made it." Instead, there was simply rejection. I was shocked! To say I was disappointed would be a gross understatement.

Devastated—that's how I felt. More like a piece of flotsam, adrift in the sea. How could this have happened? What did I do wrong? I studied hard and had gotten A's in all the subjects required for medical school, including tough classes like organic chemistry, calculus, and physiology. My professors in biology and chemistry had given me good letters of recommendation. I stayed out of trouble, and I even had a glowing letter of endorsement from the manager at the restaurant where I worked part time.

This was unprecedented (at least for me). It felt like a stiff punch to the gut. I'd never been rejected by an academic institution before. I usually thought I was the smartest guy around. Why didn't these medical schools recognize that? I found myself grappling with emotions I never knew I had. First was the denial: This can't be true. There must be some kind of mistake here. I studied hard and long, my transcripts, recommendations, and test scores were very good. Of course, after the final rejection came in, there was no denying the truth.

Then, I became almost angry. "These medical schools don't know what they are doing," I thought. "Who are they to deny me entry?" There were also feelings of embarrassment, especially when I looked around and saw fellow students who had been accepted. Were they really better than me? Why had they made it, and I hadn't been accepted? This one was really a new sensation for me and I did not like it one bit. I had to face my friends and family and tell them I had failed in my attempt. I was ashamed that I had fallen short.

Next came the depression, and this was really the worst part. I moped around, thinking, "woe is me," and feeling like a lost puppy (at least, how I imagined a lost puppy would feel). I had no focus, no direction, and no idea where to go next. Having put all my energy into the study, the tests, and the applications, I was really at a loss for my next move.

I told my family and my friends. They said, "It's okay. I'm sure things will work out for you." There was nobody in my immediate family to turn to for advice. My mother was a homemaker with six children, and my father worked for the FAA. Although they had both been to college, neither had any experience with professional education. I was the eldest child and no one I knew had been through something like this before. I didn't know any doctors or other professionals to turn to for advice.

Finally, and after much soul-searching, I reached the stage of acceptance. I hadn't been admitted into medical school. My efforts had failed. All the time spent studying and planning and the effort I had put into the application process were for nothing.

It was at this point that I began to question my decision to pursue medicine as a career. Was I really smart enough for medical school? Had I made a big mistake in trying to do this? Did the people whom I was looking to for advice really know what they were talking about? Did I have what it took to be a doctor, or was I missing something? If so, what was it? Did I really have a chance to get into medical school, or should I consider something else as a career? Why did I want to be a doctor anyway? What about medicine appealed to me at that stage of my life?

These were the questions that I asked myself day in and day out. I hadn't yet graduated college, and if medicine wasn't going to work out, I needed to develop an alternative plan.

Now it was time to take a long, hard look at the situation and make some difficult decisions. Although I didn't attach labels to my thought process back then, I went through a process that finally got me into med school and has enabled me to face many other challenges in my professional career.

The very first thing I needed to do was to make sure medical school was truly my objective.

Once I decided that yes, I did want to do this, I had to determine if it was truly within my capabilities, and for that I needed a third party's opinion. Since I did not know any physicians to whom I could turn to for advice, I turned to the next best thing—my college professors. I asked them, "Do you think I have what it takes to get into medical school and to be a good physician?" I had to trust their judgment because I had no other frame of reference. They answered, "Yes! We've seen many students over the years that have gone on to success in medical school and as doctors. We've seen your work ethic and how you work with others; we know you can do it." They believed in me, and this helped me believe in myself.

With that settled, I needed to figure out what went wrong on my first attempt and how to fix it. Was it my grades, recommendations, personal interview, experience (or lack thereof), or some intangible factor? Where had I gone wrong? I resolved to identify and fix the problem.

I knew my grades and recommendations were excellent, so I surmised that it had to be my lack of any experience working in a medical setting. Although I had worked as a volunteer in a local hospital, I had not gained much real knowledge of working with patients in that role. I applied for a job as an orderly in the emergency room; that was real medicine in action! I worked any and all shifts I could get there; as a result, I got to work directly alongside doctors and nurses with sick and injured patients. My previous thoughts about medicine as a career were confirmed. I knew this was something I wanted to do—not just from reading about it, but also from doing it.

Better yet, a doctor I worked with at the hospital asked me about my career goals. When I told him about my aspirations for medical school, he said, "I know about a volunteer position with a research neurologist at the National Institutes of Health you might look into." This was exactly the break I was hoping for! I applied and was accepted. In that position, I worked directly with a doctor who was studying neuropsychiatric disorders. I assisted him in his research and interviewed patients. In addition to the medical experience, he encouraged me in my re-application and gave me a formal recommendation.

I also returned to George Mason University where I took graduate-level courses in biology and chemistry to demonstrate my scholastic abilities. Having failed on my first attempt to get accepted, I didn't want to leave anything to chance.

Finally, I was ready to start the process again. I prepared my applications. The whole process felt much smoother and I was much more confident and relaxed during my personal interviews. I was rewarded for my efforts; instead of rejections, I began to receive acceptance letters! Not only had my efforts paid off, but also I was now in a position to decide which school best suited me and my very limited budget. I chose the University of Virginia School of Medicine and graduated from there in 1982. I went on to train in neurosurgery and completed my training in 1989.

Although my failure to be accepted into medical school on my first attempt felt awful at the time, I learned valuable lessons that have served me well throughout my training and career. They can be applied by everyone and to many situations.

First and most importantly, recognize that you never really fail unless you quit. Once the strong emotions have passed, it's time to take a logical look at your situation. You now have experience. You know what doesn't work, but you need to examine: What went right? What went wrong? Did I do something well that I can build on? Has this experience exposed areas where I am weak?

After determining your overall goals and short-term objectives, you must develop a new plan of action. Are you going to emphasize your strengths and reduce or eliminate your weaknesses? Your plan should address this. Set a deadline and tell your friends and family, if appropriate. Accountability and their support will be invaluable as you go through the process.

Finally, it's time to put the plan in action and make things happen. If you follow this outline and plan, I can almost guarantee your success.

ABOUT THE AUTHOR

Gregory Corradino, MD MBA

Education:

George Mason University, BS, Biology 1977

University of Virginia, MD 1982

Boston University Affiliated Hospitals, General Surgery 1982-84

University of Maryland, Neurosurgery Residency 1984-1989

Milligan College, MBA 2012

Gregory Corradino grew up in New Jersey and attended college and medical school in Virginia. Since completing his training in neurosurgery, he has practiced in Kingsport, TN. Recently, he has developed an interest in training new physicians in the non-medical skills necessary to succeed in professional practice. These include such topics as strategic planning, choosing partners and practices, leadership and management, communication skills, and taking an active role in building a medical practice.

He can be contacted at **g.corradino@icloud.com** or through the website **doctorstrategies.com.**

CHAPTER FOUR

Faith Rises from the Ashes
by John Bell

"For I know the plans I have for you," declares the LORD, "plans to prosper you and not to harm you, plans to give you hope and a future."

~ Jeremiah 29:11 New International Version (NIV)

On March 23, 2001, my wife Angela and I were watching the sunrise on a beautiful beach in Maui when my cell phone rang. Little did I know that this phone call was going to change my entire life. It was a neighbor from our home state, Pennsylvania, alerting us that there had been a fire at our home.

I called the police for details and found out our home had burned to the ground. The firefighters arrived on the scene to find my mother-in-law and dog outside, but Angela's father had died in the fire, along with our cat. All that remained of our home, our home office, and everything we possessed, was ashes, a stone fireplace and a chimney.

Angela and I, reeling from shock, ended our vacation in paradise abruptly and prepared to face reality. Before the fire, business had been booming. We were accustomed to living an affluent lifestyle in our beautiful contemporary home. Suddenly, we were heading home from Hawaii with four suitcases and four carry-ons, our only remaining possessions.

The downhill slide continued. We lived in an extended stay hotel until we could move into a rental property I owned. Instead of our previous privacy and seclusion, we were on the busiest street in town, bombarded by the constant sounds of sirens from ambulances, fire trucks, and police activity. Then the 9-11 terrorist attacks threw the country into a tailspin, and our business, which had already declined, deteriorated further. We were forced to use the insurance money earmarked for replacing our home just to survive.

I built new offices in our warehouse building. I researched new products and services for expanding our income. I struggled to keep work coming in. Meanwhile Angela, who had been emotionally devastated by the fire and the death of her father, developed fibromyalgia and tried to fill the void in her heart with "retail therapy," which mushroomed into a full-blown shopping addiction.

She felt the need to replace everything we had lost in the fire. We paid for storage to hold all the purchases, as we had no home. Between daily survival expenses and Angela's shopping sprees, we went through the insurance money at an alarming rate. My attempts at slowing the spending caused marital battles, further depressing her. I found myself in the ultimate no-win situation. Angela started to numb her physical and emotional pain with prescription drugs. Things spiraled downward.

Not long before the fire, I had begun a faith walk. I invested my energy in men's ministries, finding solace through practicing my faith in the workplace, with Angela, and in my relationships with friends and family. I learned more about the depth and extent of God's love for me and mankind in general, and this gave me hope.

Perhaps I was in need of perspective? My pursuit of spiritual growth helped me grow in character; I became more forgiving, empathetic, compassionate, patient, kind, and understanding. I grew in honesty and integrity. As much as I struggled, I became sure that even the tough challenges were part of God's plan. I praised Him for the work He was doing to transform me and prayed for His guidance to get us through this horrible season of life. Angela began to see changes in me and occasionally attended church with me; this encouraged me even more.

In spite of my faith, we struggled just to cover even fundamental expenses. We were awarded a huge fireproofing job by a general contractor but never received full payment for it, getting stuck for over $30,000. We couldn't afford to sue the contractor or to finish a property we had been rehabbing to sell. Our credit was ruined. We financed our home at an exorbitant rate to simply cover living expenses. I questioned God, asking, "What do You want me to learn from this?"

The financial pressure continued to mount. My old demon, anger, began to appear as my frustration ratcheted upward. Angela sank further into an abyss of endless depression. During this time, I drew more on my faith, deepening my friendship with other men in the men's ministry, finding spiritual mentors, and gaining a deeper understanding of Christ's love for us and what we are expected to do as Christians. The men held me accountable for honorable behavior in my marriage. I continued to surrender my anger to God, trusting Him to get me through this time.

I learned more about the importance of forgiving my wife and myself. I gave more control of my life to God, juggling my efforts to support my wife while struggling with mounting debt and business challenges.

Angela became addicted to the medications prescribed, which caused insomnia and increased depression. I watched helplessly as she was sucked into a massive downward vortex. I asked myself,

"What is the most loving thing I can do to support her through this time?" I reminded myself of our wedding vows and my promise to stand by her for "better or worse, in sickness and health."

As time passed, we fell behind on our mortgage payments and tried unsuccessfully to get a loan modification. Angela's behavior deteriorated from irrational to excessively compulsive, to the point where she even committed crimes. This resulted in numerous arrests, fines, and jail time, increasing the strain on our relationship and our finances. She made me promise to keep her incarceration a secret, and she concocted elaborate stories for me to tell our friends. I was forced to choose between honoring her wishes (guarding her reputation) and my desire to live an honest life. I just wanted to tell people the truth! But I also wanted Angela to get better, and I understood she needed privacy if she were ever to return to our normal life.

We didn't have enough money to finish the rehab project. As a result, I made the very difficult decision to do what is now referred to as a 'strategic default.' We stopped paying the mortgage, putting the money instead toward finishing the rehab project so we could move into that home. This strategy worked for several months, but then the bank foreclosed on us and forced us out of our home. We had 30 days to move out. I had hoped we'd have more time, since the home we were rehabbing would not be even remotely habitable for another three to four months.

My church family stepped in to provide support and manual labor. Some days I would be working on the rehab and by 8:00 am six or seven mostly-skilled craftsman would be there at my side, offering help. Amazing, right? I didn't have the money to finish paying for the kitchen or carpeting, but the church's Deacon Fund came through with funds for us. Other friends donated supplies, and by the time the 30-day deadline was up, the home was mostly habitable! Friends from church helped us pack up the old house and move into the new one.

In spite of the frustration, pressure, and stress of this situation, my faith continued to grow stronger. I became aware of the fact that I was also a sinner and was no better than Angela, even with her addictions. I felt as if I had been enlightened with the realization that actually, at heart, I was not better than anyone else. Yes, I had confessed my sins and received forgiveness by the grace of God, but I also realized I could not accept that grace and forgiveness without being willing to extend it to others. This change helped me look at the situation through a new lens, from a different perspective, and to see that Angela had a serious illness. Her addiction, compulsive shopping, and even criminal activity were all side effects that stemmed from the medications she had begun taking due to the stress of the fire and loss of her father. It was understandable. I was able to empathize with her.

As I prayed about our situation, God steered me in a manner that not only built my character, but also increased my love for Angela. As I followed this path, it became obvious that I was growing into the man God intended me to be. It became easier for me to honor and praise Him, giving Him all of the glory. I was motivated to take the love poured out on me by my church family and share that love with Angela.

Angela was in jail, about to be sentenced for a lengthy period of time. I found out she might possibly serve five-to-eight years in a state penitentiary, as a repeat offender. This possible lengthy sentence shook me to my core. I was troubled as I tried to imagine how Angela would survive such a lengthy incarceration.

I again turned to my church family. I was told about a rehab program that potentially could satisfy the judges in her case. She would serve a 30-day sentence in a faith-based program and another 30 days in a transitional unit to satisfy her full sentence. By God's grace and with His assistance, the judges accepted this alternative option and sentenced her to complete this program. I began to hope this was the beginning of her road to recovery.

Angela started the program, and over the next 30 days, each day she sounded stronger, more alive, and more coherent. I was thrilled beyond words. I longed for the day I would get back the woman I had fallen in love with and married. However, when she was transferred to the transitional housing unit, things went sideways.

Angela called to tell me she had seen a doctor who changed one of her meds, had an adverse reaction to it, and went to the emergency room. From what I was able to get out of her, they didn't do much for her at the hospital, although it was difficult to carry on a conversation with her because she was having such difficulty breathing. I talked to her numerous times that day between appointments, trying to console her and searching for ways to help her.

After my last appointment, I tried calling her and couldn't get through. I tried numerous times the next day and the following morning, but I always ended up in her voicemail. There was no number to call at the facility and I was just about to call the owner of the facility to have someone check up on her when I received another call that would change my life forever—a call from the Miami-Dade police. They had responded to a 911 call at the facility. Angela was dead.

My faith community rallied around me with emotional and financial support as I planned her memorial service and interment. I didn't have the resources to cover any of the final expenses for Angela, but the body of Christ at my church stood up and helped me to cover all of them.

Since then I have come to understand (through the many pieces of evidence she left behind) that God had been molding me, transforming me, and using me over the previous fifteen years to help get Angela ready so He could take her home. Every clue I found—notes in her Bible, a card she had sent me asking for forgiveness—reinforced this. I clung to those notes as I mourned her loss and surrendered once again to my God.

My faith walk has helped me overcome anger issues which have plagued me most of my life. God has taught me what it truly means to be a servant leader, made me exponentially more generous toward others, and allowed me to achieve a deeper level of humility than I had previously known was possible. I have become fiscally more responsible and learned that my true strength comes in acknowledging my weaknesses.

Since I lost Angela, I have remained focused on my spiritual growth. My personal life has once more begun to blossom and my business has again started to prosper. Out of the ashes of my past trials and struggles, my faith and never-give-up attitude have brought forth a flood of blessings that fuel the flames of my deepening faith, which in turn continues to benefit me. I believe God has been working on me to get me where He wants me for the next phase of my life.

I've met a Christian woman with whom I share a deep faith and consistent values. We pray daily. I am at peace with myself as I've entered into a profoundly gratifying relationship with her, keeping God at the center of our relationship. I feel loved and more alive than ever. As my business continues to grow, I'm plowing through the mountain of debt that had piled up. This all started with an unexpected phone call, at sunrise, on a beautiful beach in Maui.

If you are interested in finding peace, love, and tranquility in your life, put God first. If you want to make lasting changes in your life, ask God to help you make the transformations. If you want your ability to handle your problems to improve, try increasing your efforts to please God. Read the Bible and make your main focus pleasing Him, not anyone else. For me, God truly built something beautiful from the ashes of that fire years ago. I know He is able to help you overcome the hardships you find yourself in, no matter how hopeless they seem to be. Give God all of the praise and glory. If you do this, you will reap the rewards of faith.

ABOUT THE AUTHOR

John Bell is a much-sought-after public speaking coach, a devout Christian, a Distinguished Toastmaster, a writer, and storyteller. He has coached countless entrepreneurs, small business owners, numerous pastors, and others whose communication abilities ranged from 'terrified to speak to more than a few friends' to speakers confidently doing keynote addresses to hundreds of listeners. He specializes in helping people deliver more effective, motivational messages while keeping their audiences engaged. You may contact John via email **john@johnbbell.com**.

CHAPTER FIVE

Overflow
by Peggy McIntire

"My mind is a center of Divine operation. The Divine operation is always for expansion and fuller expression, and this means the production of something beyond what has gone before, something entirely new, not included in past experience, though proceeding out of it by an orderly sequence of growth. Therefore, since the Divine cannot change its inherent nature, it must operate in the same manner in me; consequently, in my special world, of which I am the center, it will move forward to produce new conditions, always in advance of any that have gone before."

~ Thomas Troward

In 2008 I was single, had finished raising my children, and had just received my master's degree. I was on my way. I, like everyone, had a story of triumph over many years of struggle and adversity. The saying "failure is never final" didn't have the same meaning to me then as it does today.

In December of 2007, a friend told me about a book called *The Secret* that was all the rave. I read it and saw the movie; then a light bulb went off in my head. I became excited about my newly found knowledge. I had recently spent two years trying to find a job equal to the education for which I had worked so hard, was involved in a long distance relationship that didn't seem to be going anywhere, and was not where I wanted to be in my life. Something inside of me knew that the idealism I had just read about was true, so I made a decision to put it to work.

I put in place what I call my "daily systems." Every day I gave thanks, wrote out what I was grateful for, and visualized what I wanted in my ideal life. I did whatever it took to be in a positive mood. In one year's time, I had relocated to a beautiful home with a view of Puget Sound and was living with my boyfriend, whom I loved and absolutely adored. My new business was taking off. I was living the life of my dreams. Working from my home and being my own boss. Taking walks along the beach. I had it all, or so I thought.

Four and one half years later, my life fell apart. I moved back to where I was previously living, battled legal issues regarding my failing business, and ended my relationship that turned out to be nothing I thought it would be.

I was devastated. I couldn't believe I was back to ground zero. I had gone through much in my life and had always been proud of my ability to bounce back, but this series of failures brought me to my knees.

As a result, I sank into in a deep depression for two years. I kept going over all the questions of "Why did this happen to me?" and "How did this happen?" I felt I was going crazy.

After a time of self-reflection, feeling angry, and wanting to place blame on others, I had to admit my shortcomings. I knew I had to do something.

Once again, I started each day by giving thanks. It was difficult, but I forced myself to do this despite feeling that I had nothing to be thankful for. Looking back, I can see that I had so much to be grateful for, and yet, in the moment, I could not see that.

One day after giving thanks, I became frightened. I realized I didn't feel a thing. I was an empty shell. There was no movement or energy moving through me, something I used to experience. My old religious beliefs kicked in and I wondered if this was what was meant by the phrase, "God will stop knocking at your door."

Logically, I knew I had to just keep on doing what I was doing, so I added visualizing to my daily routine. Unfortunately, I was at war with myself emotionally, and things continued to worsen. A relationship with a family member fractured, and another relationship that I thought was a salvaged relationship disappeared from my life without a word or reference to my concern. My continued legal issues made me feel ashamed and caused me to question all the years of working in a service-oriented industry. I became angry and readied myself for a fight to win back my life.

What I was doing didn't seem to be helping. I knew I needed support, guidance, and knowledge, but most importantly, experience, so I sought out someone with a great track record. I began a self-improvement course with Bob Proctor, one of the most respected and experienced self-improvement educators today. I admit it took some time, as the program is intense, but I hung in there and immersed myself in his teachings.

I became hungry for knowledge; I wanted to know myself and once again be happy. I embarked on a quest to find and study other materials as well. It took months before I started feeling like my old self, but what a revelation I had! When you hit rock bottom, you don't realize how you have let all the things you once enjoyed slip away. But, most importantly, I learned valuable lessons about my character and behaviors. Don't misunderstand. Although giving gratitude is one of the most powerful tools you can use to improve your circumstances, I needed education regarding the process through which we think and act each day. Understanding and becoming aware of the beliefs and/or baggage hidden away in my subconscious mind that drove my actions (or, rather, my inaction) is what helped me to see the things I needed to change in myself.

It's easy to say you believe in something or talk about what you want to do. But making a concrete decision and being very clear in your mind as to what you want takes time and real thinking. With focus and intention, I began to understand what it was going to take and what I had to give up in order to accomplish what I set out to do. I also realized this process was not going to be as easy as I originally thought it would be, but I was ready.

I knew, just as I did all those years ago after reading "The Secret," that my true passion was to educate and teach in the self-improvement industry and be involved in creating a new way of educating in our school system so children could learn how to be real thinkers and become the people they were meant to be. How different and wonderful our world would be! Even though my knowledge was expanding and I was exploring and dabbling in the various avenues that were presented to me, I still had not made a definite decision to begin the real work. I would be happy and determined for a while, but then out of nowhere I'd be just blah. At a standstill.

This frustrated me. I just couldn't reach that place I thought I should be. You know what I mean—that place where you are happy and productive. That place where you can see the light at the end of the tunnel and the direction you are going. Why couldn't I stop having those negative thoughts? What was wrong with me? I was doing all this studying, giving thanks, and performing my daily practices, but then bam!

Suddenly, things started happening. I had made a habit of turning on the TV and listening to music or a program for background noise, and one day a ministry program came on. It caught my attention as the minister was speaking about letting go of all the garbage that we obsessively think about. He shared a story about a time when he forgot to pack more than one pair of socks (when traveling). While on the flight home, he took off his shoes to relax. His wife commented on how much his feet stank. He was surprised because he did not notice the smell himself—the point being that when we hold onto all that garbage and continue to talk about or think about our problems, we don't realize how much we may stink to the people around us.

Later, while I was travelling for business, I started having negative thoughts. I was alone in my hotel room taking a shower, so I said out loud "you stink, you stink" and I began to laugh at what a wonderful diversion it was. Only an hour later, I was listening to a webinar with Bob Proctor, and he began talking about how all of us are not perfect and we all have our moments of negative thoughts, just as he did even though he had been practicing for over 50 years. He pointed out that you can change your focus in a short amount of time if you only practice. I knew the universe was working on my behalf.

The real revelation came the following weekend when I was watching a live stream event of *The Science of Getting Rich* with Bob Proctor. He was talking about the divinity given to us to choose our thoughts and our ability to create whatever we want. While he was speaking, I suddenly had a surge of energy go right through my body. The only way I know to describe it is that it felt like an infusion of knowledge and love. It was so powerful that I just started crying like a baby.

I was suddenly aware that I had this incredible power within me and said out loud, "Yes, you *can* do this and you *will* do this." At that moment, when I looked up again to the screen, I saw him standing on the stage looking down. He spoke out loud, but he was speaking to himself. He said, "Who said that?" I couldn't believe what I was hearing! I wondered if he actually felt what had happened to me and heard what I said! He then continued his lesson, pointing to his temple with his index and middle finger and saying that you can do whatever you want to if you use your own thoughts. It felt as though he were speaking directly to me.

I determined right there and then what I wanted and that I was going to make my dreams come true. I didn't know how I was going to get there, but I knew the answer would come.

Every day after that I kept busy. I studied, and continued my daily systems of writing out my dreams, visualizing what I wanted, giving thanks with real emotion, sending love to those who hurt me, meditating, and doing whatever I could to stay in a happy mood. Ideas flew at me. Doors opened for me. I had conversations with people who later played pivotal roles in my life. I felt happy.

I finally understood my subconscious mind was not as powerful as I always believed it to be. All my beliefs, both good and bad, created my emotions, which influenced my actions. It was revolutionary to realize that the true power was in my conscious mind; this meant I could control it. I could choose my own thoughts. I did not have to follow the opinions of others or remain a prisoner to the beliefs that did not serve me well. I was now prepared for those moments of doubt and ready to make my dreams come to fruition.

If someone were to ask me if there was just one thing they could do to change their life or help in an unpleasant situation, my answer would be to give gratitude every day. In the morning (before you do anything else), sit quietly and write out 10 things for which you are grateful. As you write, see it in your mind as vividly as possible (movement is always good).

Let's say you want a better job or to derive more enjoyment from your work. Imagine yourself at work and your boss asking you for advice or congratulating you for a job well done. When you do this, use as many of your senses as you can. Taste, smell, touch, and sound. Most importantly, visualize your goals until you truly feel emotions related to your dreams.

Remind yourself that the universe is a loving and unbiased universe. It doesn't matter where you are or where you have been. See it, feel it, be grateful for it, and believe it. That's all you have to do. The universe just recently started delivering insight, creativity, and new opportunities I never dreamt possible.

The devastation I once experienced has led me to this very moment. I'm loving myself again and am launching a consulting business, an affiliate marketing business, and I am co-authoring this book. The knowledge and message I am sending to you is this: *Failure is never final*. Visualize what you want, make a decision, take action, and your cup will overflow.

ABOUT THE AUTHOR

Peggy McIntire MSW has worked in the social service industry for the past 20 years, working with both young and elder adults. She has served as an interpreter for deaf students in all levels of education, provided nursing services at the Veterans Administration, and has worked as a hospice social worker and owner of a guardianship business. She volunteered as a court-appointed special advocate for children and internships with the Center for Justice and Homeless Veterans Center. Currently she is the owner and CEO of McIntire Affiliates and a consultant with the Proctor Gallagher Institute. Her dream is to teach the universal laws worldwide and help develop education programs using the universal laws for children. You can reach her at **peggy@asamancreates.com.**

CHAPTER SIX

Mulligans
by Dr. Jill Fjelstul

"This too shall pass."

~ Medieval Levent Proverb

I was brought up to be a golfer. My whole family golfed. I literally had a club in my hand at age two and played in my first golf tournament at age four.

Golf came naturally to me. Don't get me wrong; my future success with golf resulted from a lot of hard work. I invested numerous hours pounding golf balls on the driving range, participating in practice rounds and tournament play, studying the game, and working with sports psychologists.

The game of golf even helped me with life skills. It taught me how to strategize. Through the game, I mastered the skill of keeping my emotions in check, partially because of the mandates my parents issued as I trained and competed! I learned how to accept defeat with grace, and I learned how to turn defeat into success through action.

I also figured out how to win at the junior level, high school level, and collegiate level. Because of this success, I was faced with the decision to either make a run at becoming a professional tour player or to keep golf as part of an alternate career path. I chose the latter. I pursued the teaching and coaching side of golf and joined an industry-recognized professional golf association. My goals were to better my teaching and coaching and to become a respected and accredited professional golf teaching pro.

I successfully passed all the requirements necessary to become an apprentice member, including a playing ability test, a teaching observation test, and an academic test. A member's status with the golf association elevates with advanced testing, certification, accrual of time, and earned certification credits. Knowing this, I truly became a steward of the game. It is quite possible that my level of dedication was the precursor to the emotionally charged turn of events that anchors my story.

This is what happened.

My next level certification exam was scheduled. As expected, I diligently prepared for the test. There was no doubt in my mind that I was ready since I had prepared extensively. I drove four hours to the host test site feeling positive and confident. Not complacent or cocky, just well prepared.

Testing at this level of certification is a dynamic and demanding process. Baseline competencies are required for a successful examination outcome, regardless of the scenarios given during testing. I completed my testing with certainty that I had successfully passed the strenuous and comprehensive exam. Yes, I had made a few missteps, but nothing of concern.

Boy, was I wrong! I failed my certification exam.

I remember that day vividly. In fact, I can virtually bring myself back to that very moment. When the reviewers delivered the news that I had failed the exam, my emotions shut down. I went numb. The reviewers were talking, but I did not hear the individual words. The only thing I could process at the time was that I had failed. I got into my car and drove the four hours home, empty. In shock.

The reviewers advised me to take some time before I retested. Time passed. Negative emotions ruled my inner world. I was devastated. Embarrassed. Mad. Even little things triggered anger. For example, I continued to receive announcements, emails, and mailings from the association as if everything was fine. Yes, I knew I wasn't the only person who had ever failed the exam, but from my vantage point, why did "I" have to keep getting communications from the association that just failed me. Talk about a constant reminder of my failure!

From the association's perspective, I was still an active member. However, I didn't view myself as an active member. My thoughts about my future in golf were pale at best. How was I going to continue pursuing my professional aspirations when I had just failed an important exam in the process? I wasn't, plain and simple.

After giving it some thought, I made a conscious decision to put an end to my status with the association. I was closing that chapter of my life. I was done. It wasn't that I was content about my decision; all I could feel was total defeat.

In hindsight, I now realize that I was unable to see the big picture at that time. I simply was blind to my options. I could retest; that was standard policy. But I wasn't able to process this important fact; I blocked this very significant option.

I was so immersed in my failure that all I could feel was pure devastation. And I certainly wasn't trusting one of my favorite quotes, "This too shall pass."

Time continued to pass, but the emotional toll on my failing the exam remained with me. I couldn't let it go; I continued to obsess about it. I couldn't shake the nagging feeling that I had failed and my future plans had been stripped away.

I repeatedly relived the events leading up to the exam. I had prepared diligently and thoroughly. I was ready. I kept asking myself, "How could I have failed?"

It wasn't as if I'd never failed before. I'd lost golf tournaments and had plenty of bad shots or off days—every golfer experiences those things! However, this defeat was different. I couldn't move beyond it. In the past, I knew how to accept defeat and to overcome defeat, especially when my struggles dealt with golf. I also knew how to keep my emotions in check, but something different happened this time. I didn't know why but my emotions were clouding my judgment. Not once did I think about fighting back and retaking the exam. I chose to quit instead of strategize. I fixated on the fact that I had prepared to the fullest extent and wasn't successful. What more could I do? What could I improve upon? I didn't have answers, so I stopped searching for solutions. There was no plan B.

Then the realization of what I had done hit me. I received my member status update in the mail. I had the ultimate decision to make. There was a built-in timeframe that a member could retake a failed exam, and that deadline was fast approaching. If I didn't sign up for a retake exam within a specified period, my membership would become inactive. The very sport, the activity, that "thing" that was such a huge and important part of me throughout my entire life would be gone. My dreams and goals of staying a part of the professional association as a proud, active, and contributing member would also be gone.

I was forced to make a decision. In retrospect, it was probably good that a timeline was set because I would not have made the decision in a timely manner if it had been left up to me. The easy decision was, and had been, to do nothing. And to put it into a golf analogy, I was faced with the following decision: Was I going to use the mulligan given to all members in retaking a failed exam or quit? A mulligan is not an official rule of golf. A mulligan, by simplistic definition, is a redo. On the golf course, if you don't like a golf shot, you take a mulligan and hit again as if the first shot didn't happen. A mulligan gives you a chance to experience improvement.

It was decision time. Was I going to retake the exam or not? I needed to get a grip on my future, plain and simple. There was no doubt I was experiencing a tremendous career setback. But was I really going to pass up a retake, my mulligan, because of pride? No! I decided then and there that I was going to take back some of my power in the situation. The policy was set in place for this very situation. Why should I not take advantage of it? I could do this!

All of a sudden, things began to change for me. I instantaneously felt different. I had hope again. From the time I failed the exam to just before I chose to take my mulligan, I felt like I was helpless, out of control, when actually, I was in control the whole time. I just chose the path that did not catapult me forward.

I applied for the retake exam. I chose to accept my mulligan. I made the decision to not allow my failure to be final, and it felt good. I needed to own it from this point forward and control my destiny.

I began some deep and honest reflection once I made the decision for the retake exam. This was tough. There was an undercurrent of pressure at all times because I knew I had only one retake opportunity. I also knew how much I had prepared for the first exam. I am, however, a strong believer that nothing in this world is coincidental. I began to contemplate the possibility that I was supposed to experience this failure as a life lesson.

I jumped right in and with full force. I deeply analyzed all the variables leading up to my failed certification exam. I looked inward; I looked outward. I had previously convinced myself that I couldn't prepare any better than I had the first time around. But I was wrong. I prepared to the extremes for the retake, challenging myself physically, mentally, and academically, and well beyond the level of my first attempt preparation. I set up numerous practice teaching scenarios. I exhausted every possible scenario that I would face.

When the time came to retake the test, I felt that I was ready. I knew this was it. I had a true sense of the gravity of my situation; after all, I only had one retake.

But I was ready. Without a doubt.

My retake test site was an eight-hour drive from home, not the easy four-hour commute I drove for my first exam. I remember being incredibly nervous but ready to perform. I had a sense of peace with the day's process because somehow, through this process, I had come to grips that life would continue regardless of the outcome. This was not just a safety net for my feelings, some sort of sense of denial or sticking my head in the sand. I was truly content, knowing I would be okay at the end of the day.

The test was grueling. Anticipation was high, as it should have been. I got through it, remaining confident without dwelling on a negative outcome. Instead I focused on the requirements of each portion of the test, forcing myself to stay in the present and do my best.

The reviewers began the post examination conversation with my results.

I passed!

A tremendous weight was lifted off me, and I actually started breathing again. I had passed. Immediately, I began looking toward the future, finally planning again. This was in sharp contrast to the emotional load I'd been carrying. But now that I had passed, I could return to my original goals and the underlying reasons why I had joined the professional association many years prior.

My goals were achieved a little later than expected, but I'm glad I persevered. As ironic as this may be, I was later asked and served as an advisory board member for the very association that at one time gave me a no pass. As for career opportunities, my advanced certification has been instrumental in my professional credibility, reputation, advancements, and recognitions.

As distance has grown from my horrific experience of that first exam failure, I realize today that I value my accreditation much more than I would have, had I not endured and overcome my setback.

It is my belief that sharing personal journeys of overcoming failures offers insight and hope to those seeking to achieve the same. With this in mind, I will conclude by asking you three questions that I commonly ask myself when faced with adversity. These three questions may assist and/or control how your "failure is never final" story will end.

First, what actions are you willing to take to achieve success? It's decision time. It's time to come to grips with whatever didn't go your way, plain and simple.

Second, is achieving success your priority? You must elevate your pursuit of success to priority status. Life will get in the way. You must expect the unexpected. But if success is truly your priority, everything else will be shadowed by your pursuit of achievement.

When the going gets tough (and most likely it will), dig deep and persevere like no other time in your life. It will be worth it! I know. I've been there. Remember, I was pre-qualified to share my message in this book because I have also overcome. I made a conscious decision to succeed and I persevered.

And third, what will success feel like once you achieve it? Achieving success is tremendous. For me, I regained confidence. I finally closed that dreadful chapter in my life. My failed exam no longer clouds my mind. I finally was able to let it go. I moved on and experienced much more than my original goals.

In closing, just remember: Life is filled with mulligans. Take advantage of your mulligans. You are worth it. Invest in yourself and do it now!

ABOUT THE AUTHOR

Dr. Jill Fjelstul is a college professor, scholar, journal editor, and public speaker. She is also the author of *The Power of Belief, How Finding Your Gizmo Jump Starts Your Success*. Dr. Fjelstul is a 2015 inductee into the University of Northern Iowa's Hall of Excellence, a 2001 inductee into the University of Northern Iowa's Athletic Hall of Fame, earned her doctorate in 2006, and has been a member of the LPGA Teaching and Club Professionals since 1988. Dr. Fjelstul is a widely recognized author and speaker on RV trends and patterns and is an avid RVer and sports enthusiast. Dr. Fjelstul can be contacted at **drjillfjelstul@gmail.com** and at **www.jillfjelstul.com**.

CHAPTER SEVEN

The Wisdom of Failure
by Darrin O. Thomas

"The world needs the power of your life fully lived."

~ John Eldredge

The water looked cold.

I knew it was. I was cold. I could see my breath and it seemed to blend in with the patches of fog rising from the river below. Through the clear patches I could see a couple of black dots. I knew from experience that these dots were fisherman wading in the river near the base of the dam, hundreds of feet under the observation deck upon which I stood. Undoubtedly, they were making their final casts before the huge generators inside the dam would roar to life and the waters would rise to a torrent, making wading no longer possible.

My heart rate had already crested; my emotions raged, making rational thought impossible. A memory flashed of the last time I had waded those waters with my fly rod. That day was the closest I had ever come to actually ending my own life.

That experience had given me the idea that coming up here would be a better option. I had checked the generator schedule that day and purposefully waded into the waters when most of the other fishermen were leaving or had already left. I stayed in the water until the generator alarm sounded and the warning beacon started to flash. I lingered. I stood still in the river, leaning against the current with my eyes closed, waiting for the sensation of the cold water as it crept up my chest to the top of my waders.

It was not uncommon to hear reports of fishermen drowning here. They were either inexperienced or got too close to the generator's churn. Once the river invades your waders, it has you. You become part of it. Still, most of the stories you heard were of the flavor of the uneventful close call. That day, I had looked up to where I was now standing.

The memory was gone as quick as it had come. I stepped out to the edge of the observation deck. My legs were beginning to revolt but I forced myself to stand still. I looked around and then back down at the river. I was alone. The river was clear. I couldn't see the generators' beacon from this height, nor hear its alarm, but I knew what was happening. I was shaking in the morning air of late spring in East Tennessee, the cold piercing me despite the protection of my suit jacket. I had shaved and put on my suit like I did every morning. Except, this morning I had come here. Here to this spot high above the river.

My insides were wracked. My body trembled violently. I wiped my eyes. I had visualized this so many times in different ways and in different places. But now I was here.

I had never been this close before. I was not ready to die but I *was* ready to end the constant torment and pain of my depression. I was ready to end the indescribable daily suffocation that comes with always hiding the truth about my struggles while donning the mask of normalcy. My life was a lie. I was a fake, and I was tired of posing for everyone.

I believed my failure at life and business was complete. I was sick, but nobody knew. No one would even have guessed that my recent business and relationship failures had affected me so severely, but the reality of my failures had consumed me. It was all I could see.

Looking back now I have the objectivity to recognize that I had been dealing with clinical depression since my early twenties. Though latent for a long time, at some point my depression was triggered and had snowballed. It made me restless and started a cycle of inconsistency in my relationships and work performance that would eventually suffocate even my personality. By the early 2000s, my depression had destroyed my ability to focus and produce results. In 2003, I was fired from my high-paying job in medical sales. I tried to rebound, but my thoughts and emotions were out of control by that point. I was in the floodwaters and going down fast.

Nobody knew where I was that crisp morning above the Clinch River—physically, mentally, or emotionally. They would eventually find me, though. Either churning in the waters at the base of the dam or downstream somewhere. At that discovery, everyone would know where I was, and in every way. They would all have a good idea of who I really was. Everyone who knew me or cared about me would know that I wasn't who they thought I was, and I would be unable to change that treacherous and tragic exclamation point on my life.

While standing on that observation deck, I asked myself, "What if everyone else knew now? Would I be able to recover from that revelation?"

"What if only a few people really knew where I am at right now and what I am dealing with? Then would I be able to recover?"

"What if only one person knew, and that revelation was enough to save me?"

I thought about my beautiful wife, Sabrena. She loved me, unconditionally. After 11 years she had proved that she was not just committed to a perfect image of me, but that she was committed to the whole me—me as I am. Period.

I stepped off the ledge and called my wife.

A lot of what happened after that phone call still remains a bit fuzzy for me. I remember talking about my depression with my wife. As best I could, I brought her up to speed on all that had been going on with me for the past couple of years and the line of thinking that continually led me to the edge of suicide. She was blown away by what I told her, I am sure of that much.

We cried together and talked about what to do next. We agreed that there was a way forward, even if we didn't fully see it yet. We also agreed that God had given me, and us, a second chance. We were not going to take it for granted or waste it.

I went to see my medical doctor first thing. He diagnosed me with clinical depression and prescribed medication and counseling. He went a step further and gave me his cell phone number and made me promise to call him if I got to the point of suicidal ideation again.

Once the medication started working, I gained some much-needed clarity. It was like I had been living under a sheet of ice in a frozen lake and only sporadically was able to find small pockets of air, each pocket affording me only small gasps before I was thrust back underwater. Now, thanks to the medication, I had a hole in the ice. I could stick my head up above the water line and finally breathe deeply. I then found a great psychologist who helped me climb the rest of the way out of the lake.

I continued the two therapies my doctor had prescribed for eighteen months. Each day brought more objectivity, clarity, and healing. I started to look for ways to accelerate my recovery, and through that seeking process, I discovered the amazing world of personal development. I devoured everything I could find related to goal setting, faith, belief, and the power of subconscious thought. I was drawn to some of the pillars in the teaching of personal development, in particular, Napoleon Hill, Robert Collier, Brian Tracy, James Allen, and Vic Johnson. Under their patient mentorship, I re-learned how to think, believe, and dream. I began to live in the moment and let my closest relationships and the sanctity of my own life define my self-worth. I regained hope and renewed my creative enthusiasm for life and business.

I was still an employee during this period of healing. While my personal recovery was going great, my relationship with my employer was beyond repair. I was given the wonderful opportunity to resign my position—instead of being fired. I bought myself three more months, which enabled me to start my first business, a digital marketing company, in April of 2006. The business was actually growing until the economic downturn decimated our market and put us out of business around the end of 2008. Still, I was not deterred. Instead of getting discouraged, I refer to that experience as my MBA in Business Street Smarts. I have learned more from that single failure than from any other experience in my career. Any success I have had since then can be directly credited to that failure. Sure, I had to endure some negative consequences like debt and lack of income. However, these trials were a small price to pay for what I have gained from the experience.

From that newly formed but firm foundation, solidified by personal development and real-world business experience, I have launched four consecutive businesses. In 2008, I started consulting, which led to one of my clients hiring me to act as CEO of their company. In 2011, I left that CEO position to start my own medical sales company, which made $1.5 million in its first 30 months. In 2014, I utilized some of the profits from that venture to start a medical laboratory with two partners, which is now doing about $4 million in annual revenue. In the fourth quarter of 2015, alongside my original partner and brother, James, I re-started the digital marketing firm that had failed in 2008. We re-branded, niched our service, and are planning to launch in seven U.S. cities this year.

I have learned so much in all of this, but several of the lessons I have learned in the past 20 years go much deeper and have delivered significant benefits in far greater ways than mere business principles ever could.

One thing I have learned is that failure is more friend than foe. I now like to think that, given the choice between sure success and possible failure, I would choose the path that left me exposed to failure. I have to humbly admit that failure has been a much more loyal and exacting mentor than success has been, but the things that failure has taught me have affected changes in the core of my nature. I can't say that about the things I have learned from success. As much as I want to succeed, the dividends of success are somehow temporal compared to the checks that failure writes. Please don't get me wrong here. I am in business and in life to succeed. I have never set out to fail. Yet, I have come to realize and appreciate something very important. Every time I plan, failure is right there instructing me and honing my tactics. Every time I take action, failure is right there keeping me honest and making me more effective. Every time I have a win, failure is reminding me that wins aren't easy or sure.

I have also learned that life and business will always have their ups and downs. This is natural, and we will all do well to get this into our brains. To remain on track, I remind myself that I should not be surprised or caught off guard by this. I still get down, but I am always moving forward with the knowledge that I am no longer defined by failure or success in any aspect of life. Naturally, my life is not problem-free, and in weak moments I still sometimes wish away obstacles and setbacks. However, I quickly remember that if the problems of life could be wished away, this would not be real life. It would not be MY life!

Finally, and most importantly, the world needs you to live your life to its fullest potential. The world does not just need you to simply exist; it needs the full expression of who you are. I really believe that you were created on purpose and with a purpose. Your purpose fits into the whole scheme of creation and is a necessary part of the whole.

Maybe you have faced a major setback. Maybe you are in the middle of dealing with one right now. Maybe you are on the other side of failure, but you are allowing that setback to define you.

Maybe you are out on the ledge right now, like I once was. Please step back. Your failure contains the greatest potential positive force for your life. Let it propel you forward.

ABOUT THE AUTHOR

Darrin O. Thomas lives in the Indianapolis, Indiana area with his beautiful wife Sabrena and their two children. He has a 17-year track record of do-it-yourself entrepreneur-ship and currently oversees three of his business creations: a multi-million dollar medical lab, a national medical marketing company, and the #1 SEO Firm in Indianapolis: IndianapolisSEO.org (an SEOTyrants.com property).

Darrin has a passion to speak to groups who are looking for new ways to break through to greater success in accomplishing their mission and purpose. Contact him at **Darrin@SEOTyrants.com** about providing motivational and visioneering services for your business or non-profit group.

CHAPTER EIGHT

I Didn't Know I Didn't Know
by Dean Mannheimer

"If you want to have more, you have to become more. For things to change, you have to change. For things to get better, you have to get better. For things to improve, you have to improve. If you grow, everything grows for you."

~ Jim Rohn

When I was much younger I lived in my own world, thinking I was part of the real world. Later in life, a friend described to me that I was "living in an egg." Essentially, I had "learned to paint the inside of the egg to look like the outside. There was sky above me and grass I walked upon. All the details were there, but it was still only the inside of the egg."

When I describe my life in this way, I mean I was running my life and business without really understanding what principles and disciplines were necessary for true victory. I had allowed my early success to delude me into thinking I was responsible for my accomplishments.

Then, one day, reality hit. The eggshell cracked wide open.

It was not until on a Monday morning in March 1986 that I realized I was not going to be able to make payroll for my business. Subsequently, over the following few weeks, I came to the realization that I was going to lose my business and everything I had gained financially in life up to that point. As you can imagine, this was a mind-blowing realization.

While going through the process of losing my business, I saw that while there are many times when the court system does not move quickly, my business bankruptcy was not one of those times. It happened all too soon. I locked the door to my business for the final time on a warm Wednesday afternoon, a day that felt surreal. I had been going through the motions with my attorney, but I had not let my emotions really take hold of me until that moment when I turned the key in the lock for that last time. Suddenly I felt like I had just been punched in the stomach, only I didn't think I was ever going to be able to catch my breath. It was as if all the time it took to go through the process had caught up to me in that instant.

I felt like I had lost everything that made my life worth living. I had no business, no savings (basically, no money), no job, and no idea what I was going to do. Going through bankruptcy was devastating in every way—financially, emotionally, and psychologically. Life was very dark for me then. Up until that point, I defined my value by money, status, title, and how other people perceived me.

This last point—how people perceived me—played especially nasty games with my psyche. Having failed with my business, I believed people perceived me as a failure.

Someone to pity. Not capable of providing for my family. I thought they viewed me as a second-class person.

I believed I had let everyone down, and that belief paralyzed me. I had no idea that I had my priorities all wrong. In hindsight, I can say that experience was a stepping-stone for me, but at the time, I was unable to see how I might grow from this time. As a result, I sunk into a very low emotional place.

At the time, I did not realize that my emotional growth had been stunted early on by the way I was educated in business. I was taught business came first, including before my moral compass, family, or health. I was taught that you can lose everything and still move forward—as long as you still have your business, because your business was the top priority.

I sat in my home, which I had not yet lost, and listened to the quietness. The kids were in school and my wife was working a part-time job, so I had time to think. For weeks I did that and nothing else: sat in the silence and pondered my situation.

Finally, I snapped out of it and came to the realization that I had to do something. If things were to change, I had to make some decisions. At that point, I thought there were only a couple of real options available to me. One of the options I was entertaining during my darkest hours had to be crossed off immediately; it was not truly an option.

I needed to start making money so I could buy food and pay some of the personal bills. I needed to look at job possibilities. Over the next few weeks, I did just that, and I found a job that at least matched some of the skills I had at the time and allowed me to move forward a little. It was a semi-management role for a small chain of pet supply stores. I worked in that job while I went through the rest of the fallout that comes from a bankruptcy. If you've never been through a bankruptcy, you'll need to just trust me when I say there was plenty of that. We had to move from our home to a small rental. We lost our cars and most everything of value. But between the income I was earning and what my wife was making, we were able to pay for the bare essentials to get by for a while.

I had hoped that working would help me recover, but even the job was not enough. My male ego would not yet let me change my feelings about my capabilities. I had lost the ability to trust my own judgment, and along with that, I had lost my sense of self-worth. That put me in a mental frame of mind that prevented me from moving forward in a meaningful way. When imprisoned in a mental cage, it is difficult to break free.

I had never experienced this kind of mental trauma because I had lived what I thought was a charmed life until this happened. That meant I was not prepared to deal with all that was happening to me. I was so beat down that I reached the point that is often referred to as hitting rock bottom. I had to be so low that the only direction for me to go was up. That was when I finally accepted the concept of a new start.

The first thing I needed to do was change my attitude. I was at a place in my life that I didn't like spending time with myself. I accomplished this by listening to motivational tapes and attending seminars by successful people. The tapes dealt with both personal issues and business problems. Many of the tapes and seminars taught me that the obstacle was never the problem I faced but rather how I went about dealing with problems.

I learned several key concepts that transformed my perspective. For starters, everything in life is a process. There are ups and downs, highs and lows, and there is much to be learned from every experience.

At one seminar I listened to a speaker, Denis Waitley, talk about loss. He said, "There are two primary choices in life: accept conditions as they exist, or accept the responsibility to change them." That struck home with me; it was a pivotal concept that altered how I thought about difficult situations. I realized that life (and all that it includes) is like your heartbeat as seen on the doctor's electrocardiogram. The beat goes up, down, up, and then down again. It always continues on in that fashion. When the machine shows a heartbeat as a flat line, it means the person has died. The author's point was that everything in life is like a heartbeat, so why would you want life to be a flat line? If it was flat, you are no longer among the living. That made a lot of sense to me.

I realized I was not as smart as I thought I was. My ego had gotten in the way of my learning basic facts about living life. By that I mean I did not know what I did not know. I was so ignorant of the principles of business that I did not know which questions to ask. When that revelation struck me, I was able to learn by reading books that taught me these basics I had previously been unable to comprehend.

I began attending seminars and lectures by successful people, and as I did, it struck me that all of these people had also gone through their own hard times. That right there was the single most important step for me. I found out I was not alone in a failure of a business, or, more importantly, my struggles with self-worth. I also learned that this was going to be a process for me. Nothing was going to happen overnight. I did not get to where I was overnight and I was not going to get out of it that way either.

I had heard it said that half the solution to a problem is realizing there is one. Now I knew I had a problem. I strove to identify viable options—actions I could take that would be productive. Starting another business was out of the question because I had no money. Working with a partner did not seem to be a good idea at the time. Finding a job that would pay me what I believed I should earn would take years to achieve—and in that there were no guarantees.

Being at the point I was, I realized the best option for me was to be entrepreneurial. It allowed me to mentally explore multiple options and opened some doors for me that had previously been closed. I started investigating everything possible. I read the want ads, not only for other jobs but also for other kinds of opportunities. I started to see there were in fact many different types of opportunities, and that many of those options would not cost me a bunch of money. There were investors with money looking for talented people to put to work. Mentally, that might have been a stretch for me, but my point is that new doors began opening.

I ultimately came across a business opportunity that allowed me to stay in business for myself but did not have any of the traditional liabilities attached to it. I selected one of those businesses while I kept my existing job (so I could pay the bills). I finally came to appreciate the prudence of being conservative.

While I was going through this process of defining and refining myself, I needed to find a new career path. I also had to change (or I should say re-establish) the correct priorities for my life. The principles and processes I was learning would also apply to my personal life. I shifted my understanding that my life was to be defined by the following:

1. My moral compass, my faith
2. My family
3. My health
4. My business

During the time I was rebuilding, I worked hard to ensure that I did all I could to avoid making the same mistakes. I understood the premise that a balanced life would enable me to become more attentive to my business, my family, my health, and my faith.

This is what I suggest you take from my experience (and the experiences of the successful people I have met through my journey): Know that you are not defeated unless you give up and quit. What you go through today will prepare you for many of the challenges you will face later. There is no disgrace in a defeat, but there is disgrace in giving up.

A friend of mine says the harder he gets knocked down, the higher he bounces. If you are not stretching to grow as you face challenges, you will not develop the mental tools you need to live a fulfilling life. Accept the challenges and the temporary defeats, and you will realize that anything else life throws at you are merely opportunities to get better.

There is no such a thing as "failure is final." The only time anything is final is when you allow something to be final. The real final aspect of your life will be when you have taken your last breath here on earth and go to meet your maker. That will truly be final; anything else is an inconvenience.

ABOUT THE AUTHOR

Dean Mannheimer was born September 3, 1949 and is married with two children and three grandchildren. He attended Arizona State University.

After university, Dean spent 15 years with a regional mass merchant chain based in Arizona. He rose through the ranks of management quickly to eventually become their general merchandise manager for what was called their hard-lines division. He learned much of his management skills working for this chain.

Dean decided to branch out on his own and left the retail chain. He went into partnership with a couple of friends and entered the restaurant business. While still in partnership in the restaurant business, Dean also bought a fabricating company as a finish contract in the home building business. He owned these businesses for five years before changing career paths.

Dean sold his partnership in the restaurant business and closed his fabricating business to concentrate on his new career.

Dean has been in the direct sales industry for 25 years, traveling the globe building and training tens of thousands of independent business owners. He has helped many earn seven figures a year and hundreds earn six figures a year.

Dean has spent the last number of years teaching people how to run their businesses and motivate their people.

CHAPTER NINE

The Stranger Named Bill
by Jeff Spedding

"As a man thinketh, so is he, and as a man chooseth, so is he."

~ Ralph Waldo Emerson

Have you ever met a young man whom, if given the right opportunities, you were sure would be a success in life?

If ever there were such a person, that would've been me. At eight years old, I already had a number of small businesses going: newspaper route, gardening, door-to-door candy sales, and any other small jobs I could find. I was making more money than boys two or three times my age.

Then, at the tender age of 12, my life took a turn for the worse and started on a long, downward spiral. I lived in a seemingly normal middle class home with a dad, a mom, two sisters, and a brother. From all outward appearances, you would think our home was nothing out of the ordinary. However, behind closed doors there was physical, sexual, and mental abuse going on. My older brother was molesting me and teaching me behaviors that were not in line with my preferences; however, I was so lonely and afraid that I allowed it to happen. My parents were wrapped up in their own personal issues, so they were not paying attention to the kids. This abuse was my shameful secret; I did my best to hide it from my friends.

In this state of physical and emotional torment, one day some of my peers offered me some beer and marijuana. I discovered the substances numbed the pain of feeling different from the other boys. After that, I started to use on a regular basis, and within a very short period time, I became an addict.

My addiction took me on a 25-year slide down to the depths of hell, using every kind of substance available. Drugs, alcohol—you name it, I tried it. I barely finished high school.

I was a pretty good auto mechanic, so I was fairly successful at getting jobs. Keeping them was a different story. I went from shop to shop, staying only as long as my employers would put up with my tardiness and absences. Over time, my skills deteriorated, so even my performance was not as good as it once was. I had to move often because I was usually unable to pay my rent. I was using all I could earn on drugs. I ended up in jail more times than I can remember.

This continued until one day I crash-landed in an emergency room in cardiac arrest from an overdose. I awoke in a hospital bed, not entirely glad to find myself alive. As you might imagine, at this stage of my life, I was completely bankrupt, not only financially, but mentally and spiritually as well. I had alienated my friends, my family had given up on me, and any woman who had ever put up with me was long gone. I was homeless, unemployable, and all alone. My life was a mess, and I couldn't see how I would ever find my way out of this hellish existence.

The hospital stay brought with it a shower, a clean bed, and free, hot meals; but it also brought something else I hadn't expected. That episode was the beginning of the end of my self-consuming addiction.

Later that day, a social worker named Patty came into my room and asked if I would like some help in turning my life around. Ordinarily, I would have shut her out. I wasn't in the habit of pouring out my problems, which in my mind I didn't really have, to perfect strangers. But that day, I didn't do what I would have ordinarily done. I had come to the realization that I couldn't go on this way any longer; as a result of this, I was willing to try anything. Not knowing exactly what I was in for, I agreed to whatever she was offering.

Patty wasn't able to work with me personally, but as a social worker, she had a wealth of resources. She contacted a man named Bill who had overcome his own dependency problem and now worked as a pro bono rehab specialist. She'd seen Bill work with many guys in similar situations, so she figured he could handle a hard case like me.

Bill came to my hospital room and Patty introduced me to my first mentor. Although I didn't realize it at the time, that day I embarked on a journey that rocketed me from failure to fortune in a very short time. That may sound like a dramatic turn-around, which it truly was. I'll tell you what made it possible for me to go from homeless to successful in the hope that you will glean some sort of inspiration or lessons that you can apply to your life.

Although I'd agreed to work with Bill, I was still a little resistant to having some know-it-all tell me how to fix my life. He didn't know how big my problems were. Bill carried himself with a kind of confidence that would usually have made me defensive, but I guess he saw through me because he immediately went to work on breaking down my defenses. He was kind and gentle, yet very sure of himself. You know the type—someone who knows who he is and is very comfortable in his own skin. I began to see how much I wanted to also be that way.

After an hour of small talk, Bill asked me, "Are you willing to follow some directions?"

Again, not knowing what I was getting into, I said, "Yes." I could already see that whatever direction Bill was going to take me had to be better than the direction I was headed on my own.

With Bill's help, I checked out of the hospital and into a recovery home. A few days later, he took me to dinner so we could explore where I had been and exactly how I'd gotten to where I was in life. He said he needed to know my past so he could help me lay out a plan of action for building my future.

Sitting in the corner booth at the little diner, Bill asked me a lot of very personal questions and actually made notes of my answers in a little notebook. This guy was serious.

After the question and answer session, Bill said, "Jeff, there are three basic principles you need to follow in order to build a successful life, and over the next 90 days, you will be working on these, with my help.

I call these principles 'the three P's to prosperity.' They are perspective, purpose, and persistence."

As we worked through those 90 days, I established myself a structure upon which I built a new life. A new life that led to financial prosperity, renewed ties with my family, and built meaningful emotional relationships. Those three principles, "the three P's of prosperity," have continued to guide me to this day. Let's look at them, shall we?

Principle One: Perspective
Bill said, "For the first 30 days, we will be working on your perspective. By that I mean your attitude about life and the way you look at things.

You see, Jeff, when you change the way you look at things, the things you look at change. And you have been looking at things from the wrong perspective."

So, once a week, I met with Bill in that same diner to go over this process. He had me write an autobiography detailing the good and bad experiences of my past. How my attitude had impacted my relationships with others and how I was affected by the preconceptions I brought into situations. He had me write down my feelings, which were, at first, numb and hard to identify. He also asked me to describe my behavior in significant relationships.

When I had finished writing all this out, we met again and went over it all together. This was a very humbling experience, but also a very cleansing one. You can kid yourself about things that you keep locked inside, but when you admit things to someone else, saying the truth out loud, you are really set free. So it was worth the slice—or, in my case, the whole pie—of humble pie one has to eat to accomplish this.

Now that a good start had been made on changing my perspective, (and, consequently, my attitude), Bill gave me my next assignment, which aligned with the second principle.

Principle Two: Purpose
In that diner booth that had become so familiar, Bill explained that the next 30 days would be spent figuring out my purpose for being.

He said, "Jeff, in order to really get anywhere in life, you have know your purpose in life. Your assignment is to create a personal mission statement. You can get a good start on this by going to **http://msb.franklincovey.com**. We will expand on this base as time goes on."

I went to the website and filled out their self-assessment questionnaire. When I had answered all the questions, I realized that I had a starting place, a foundation upon which I could build. The mission statement I developed became the solid rock on which I could build a fabulous life based on the things I had determined were truly most important to me. It had been so long since I had had a purpose! Living purposefully brought meaning back to my existence like you can't possibly imagine.

When you know your purpose in life and truly believe that all you do is good and right, you will be fired up from the depth of your being with a fuel that no amount of discouragement, heartache, or fear can extinguish. You will strive not only for the accomplishment itself, but for what the experience of seeking that accomplishment will make of you. The strength of character that you gain becomes your true success.

For most of my life, all my choices had been self-centered with no regard for anyone else's well-being. It was time to pay attention to my choices, who those choices affected, what my contribution to my relationships were, and how these actions would later make me feel.

Now, when I am blessed to take others through this process, we ask them to ask themselves these questions and write down their answers in a workbook we have created. The following are three of the questions we ask:

Q. Why do you want this to be?

Q. Who do you want to impact, and how will you do this?

Q. Who will you bring along on this journey? (You will need partners, and it's more fun doing this with a partner than doing it alone.)

Principle Three: Persistence
At the 60-day mark, Bill met me in our usual booth. This time I told him that I had found a job and I was buying. Bill grinned from ear to ear as he said, "I accept." I'm not sure if he was more pleased by my progress or by the fact that someone else was picking up the tab for a change!

That day we began to talk about persistence. Because Bill had delved into my dark past with me, he knew that in the past when things didn't work out for me the first time, I just gave up and stopped trying. He pointed out that I was never going to win if I was unwilling to do the hard work.

He said, "Listen carefully, Jeff. Winners do what they have to do. Losers do what they want, and Jeff, you're not a loser anymore."

Then he said, "It matters not if you try and fail and try and fail again. No matter what happens, you get up, brush yourself off, and go at it again. You haven't really failed unless you fail to try again. You keep trying until you have achieved your objective. That's persistence."

Persistence relates back to perspective. After setbacks, ask yourself, "Did I learn something from this attempt?" The obvious answer is, "Of course I did. I learned that that approach doesn't work, so I can cross that off as a possible solution and come at it from a different angle."

I quote Bill when I say, "failure is a stepping-stone on the path to attainment of a worthy goal, not a roadblock." You must keep on keeping on if you are going to win.

After much refinement of this process, we found the best way to monitor progress is to write down what worked and what didn't. Working with a mentor, you will get another perspective. If you don't have a mentor, do some brainstorming with your friends or family. More often than not, you are just a little off in one area or the other. Talking it out can help you discover options you didn't realize you had. A little help never hurts!

It has been my experience that it is helpful to ask myself each day, "How can I be of service to others and make a contribution for the betterment of mankind?" If you pay attention to your attitude and correct it when you find yourself in a negative mood, your perspective will change. Most importantly, if you are persistent in pursuing your dreams and passions, you will fulfill your purpose in life. This, in turn, will fill your heart and soul in ways others only dream about.

I am confident that this can work for you because it has worked not only for Bill, and for me, but also for countless others.

As you work through this process, I am confident that you will find true happiness and genuine peace in the wonderful new life you build for yourself. May God bless you and keep you until then.

ABOUT THE AUTHOR

Jeff Spedding is a very popular and highly sought after speaker, trainer, and coach who has been working successfully with groups and individuals for the past 25 years. Jeff is a successful businessman, father, husband, and community leader.

For the past 25 years, Jeff has not only accomplished every goal he set, he has far exceeded them. With a powerfully strong passion for personal growth and relentless determination, Jeff is committed to helping others grow.

Jeff's family life is also remarkable because of an altered attitude and a deeper understanding about life, love, patience, acceptance, and true tolerance. Jeff has been happily married to his kind and generous wife Anne for the past 18 years. Together, they have one remarkably independent son, Winston.

Jeff can be reached at: **jeff@jeffspedding.com**.
Visit him on the web at **www.jeffspedding.com**.

CHAPTER TEN

Finding Forgiveness and Gratitude in the Depths of My Despair Turned My Life Around

by Jennifer Barna

"Starting over can be the scariest thing in the entire world, whether it's leaving a lover, a school, a team, a friend, or anything else that feels like a core part of our identity, but when your gut is telling you that something here isn't right or feels unsafe, I really want you to listen and trust in that voice."

~ **Jennifer Elisabeth**

The darkest night of my soul was the culmination of a decade of bad boys, bad drugs, secret lives, and self-defeating life choices. It started when I ran away from home and joined the military at age 18. I returned home six months later the victim of a drill sergeant's sexual assault. I plunged into a day-night secret life of hard work by day and hard partying by night. I worked overtime to keep the people involved in my day life away from the people in my nightlife—and vice versa.

But when the drug dealer of my mentally unstable, gun-wielding ex-boyfriend showed up at work insisting I had to pay up my ex-boyfriend's debt or else, my two worlds collided. I realized I needed to exit "the life" and moved away with a man also interested in leaving "the life." Our fresh start led to marriage, a family, and a new normal for both of us.

Sadly, that fresh start deteriorated into the tired, chaotic pattern of my past. The old normal soon took over the new normal, and this time, the depths of my unhealthy pattern reached new lows.

The verbal and physical abuse had been happening for quite some time. I was physically, emotionally, and mentally cut off from the world outside the walls of our townhouse. After another terrible blowup fight, complete with the usual screaming and body blows, he left. Our children were asleep in bed, and I didn't know how long he would be gone. I cried until I felt completely empty. The hollow space in my heart reached my soul.

A quiet, dead space entered after I stopped crying. I realized I didn't know how to be happy anymore; in fact, I *couldn't* be happy anymore. I felt sorry for myself. I was fearful for my life. I was afraid to look anyone in the eye. I had little to no outside contact with the world. I had no friends to turn to and no family I was willing to tell—or admit to—that this horrible thing was happening in my life.

That was the worst moment of my life. Up to that point, I had never felt more alone, helpless, hopeless, worthless, and empty. I realized I had lost myself a long time ago and questioned, how did I end up here? I felt like I had lost the ability to love and be loved. I felt like I had failed at life.

I went to the bedroom and grabbed the sheet off the unmade bed. I wrapped one end around the top of the stairwell and the other around my neck. I walked up and down the stairs to figure out how to jump and hang myself. With my eyes puffy from crying and tears rolling down my face, I started to lift my leg over the side of the railing. The air grew still. Then I heard the slightest sound from the upstairs bedroom.

I heard my baby whimper in the night and it felt as if God himself had shook me with both his hands. God spoke to me through the whimper of my child. "I believe in you and love you. You have to protect them."

All of a sudden, I realized I had two precious little beings that chose me to be their mother. I was *needed*. I was the person responsible for protecting them, guiding them, and keeping them safe. I definitely was not meant to go out this way! Clarity and decision emerged. I looked down at what I was doing, immediately pulled the sheet off the bannister, and ran to their room. My two precious little children were sleeping soundly in their beds. I lay my hands gently on them as they slept and vowed right then and there that things were going to change.

God reminded me through those little beings that my purpose in life is to love and be loved. Where my heart and soul had been hollow, I started to recognize God's grace. In this, my darkest night by far, I was grateful to be alive. I was grateful to love my babies and be loved by them in return.

While love and gratitude were my motivation, I still had to manage the practicalities of finding a safe haven away from an abusive marriage. I was still afraid of what the next day would bring, but I now had laser-focused intent and determination.

As is often the case when we lock onto our intent, making my way to safety occurred relatively quickly. Within two weeks, my husband was arrested for spousal abuse and child endangerment. I used his arrest to move 400 miles away to be with my family. Then I began the process of starting over, yet again. This time I was a single mother with a toddler and an infant. I had no job, little education, and some family support.

What I *did* have was the burning intention to create a new life for myself and my children based on the foundation of loving and being loved. I didn't really know how this intention would manifest. I only knew that loving and being loved was at the core of who I am. I fully realized that I HAD to build my life around this core.

I have followed through with this promise.

To accomplish this goal, I have spent the better part of a decade creating the life I always envisioned. The previous three decades were a struggle between who I knew I was and who my family and friends wanted me to be. More often than not, I chose to live in accordance to the desires of my family and friends instead of staying true to my own vision for myself.

Yet, I always knew deep down inside that I could be more. I realized I could achieve more. I yearned to be around successful people to learn how they achieved the things they did. Through the help of a loving, supportive husband and the guidance of several mentors, I am not only creating the successful life I longed for as a child, but coaching others to do the same as well.

Through my mentors, I have found that my previous behavior is called "letting the outside circumstances and other people's thoughts and actions control you." I am mastering the ability to work and live from the inside out, instead of the outside in, and happily teaching others how to do this as well. This is where everyone's power lies.

A part of my healing process entailed coming to terms with key events in the past: sexual assault, verbal and physical abuse, and drug abuse. I was lucky enough to work with a special woman who became my life coach. She helped me recognize my own gifts. She taught me that my feelings about situations are more important than anyone else's opinions or feelings. She helped me focus on my role, my wants, and my power in situations.

She also helped me discover the power of forgiveness. She helped me harness forgiveness to alleviate the emotional charge I had related to these events. When I released the deep hurt and pain I carried, I was able to focus on what I really wanted in my life. I was able to finally start focusing on my future.

Shortly after working with this amazing woman, I stumbled upon a world-class master thinker, Bob Proctor, on the Internet. Through his *Six Minutes to Success* video series, I started to connect the dots to all the good (and the bad in my life), and even how I made it through much of it.

I then attended my first Bob Proctor seminar. After the weekend seminar, I was hooked. I loved his message and needed to know more. Honed over 50 years of him teaching, the principle of "we become what we think about" resonated with my very core. I applied the principle immediately, and my life really started to change dramatically.

My growth came at an exponential rate when I started to understand myself better—how my mind works and how I think. I knew that studying with Bob Proctor was integral to what I wanted to do with my life. I signed up to become a facilitator and coach of Bob's program *Thinking Into Results*.

Through Bob's training, I learned how the conscious and sub-conscious parts of our mind works, greatly affecting our behavior and our results. I realized that my early life experiences molded my beliefs and self-esteem, and my beliefs and self-image influenced the decisions I made in my early adult years. Without judgment about the past, I realized that the thoughts that had molded me as a child could be recast, and that this recasting would change the pattern of my life. I was no longer a victim of my past, but the creator of my future.

As my beliefs shifted, I became healthier and fit, having released 25 pounds. I no longer need to use narcotics for my back pain. I am less stressed and extremely happy and fulfilled. I no longer have "bad" days or "down" days. I feel an overall sense of love, joy, and wellness. My family is happier and my relationships are improved. I am making more money in a month than I ever have before. I am living the life I have always envisioned—a life that seemed so far, far away that dark night twelve years ago.

I have connected with my inner light and found my purpose. I realize that all the heartache, all the joy, all the pain, and all the healing I have experienced is not just mine—these experiences combine to form a roadmap that I can use to help others heal their hurts and change their lives.

Just as gratitude and forgiveness have played important roles in my healing process and personal growth, I am seeing these twin powers of mind also helping others. I see in myself and in others how gratitude and forgiveness show us that we can be strong, resilient, determined, happy, and loved.

Finding gratitude every day—in even the uncomfortable or unwanted things that happen in life—changes our perspectives about everything we encounter. Choosing forgiveness enables us to release regret, anger, guilt, and the hurt that holds us back. When we can come to terms with our past actions and learn how we can improve our own behavior, we build a solid foundation upon which to move forward in life. Through gratitude and forgiveness, I have made room for better people, better opportunities, and better things to come into my life.

I do not think my journey is unique. Certainly the experience has been mine. However, as I share my experience with others, I find people similarly seeking to transform their journeys of adversity into lives filled with joy, love, gratitude, forgiveness, and triumph.

With the help of divine power and the guidance of my teachers and mentors, I know now that failure is never final. We all share the power to think our lives to the success we want to experience.

Here's to your success! Cheers!

ABOUT THE AUTHOR

Jennifer Barna is a certified facilitator and coach with the Proctor Gallagher Institute, guiding people in changing their lives from where they are to where they truly want to be. She wants to help as many people as she can to live their life by design, not by default. She loves helping people light and re-light the flame in their hearts to live more successful, meaningful, and fulfilling lives. Her clients love her warm, genuine, passionate, and com-passionate nature, and the insight they receive when working with her.

She happily lives and works with her husband, two teenage sons and dog in Sacramento, California. She enjoys reading, traveling, walking along the river, movies, and continued education and training in her field. And when not following her calling, she can be found at a baseball or soccer field supporting her children.

Jen can be contacted at **www.jenbarnasuccess@gmail.com** or find her through FaceBook at Thinking Into Results Facilitator and Mindset Coach -Jen Barna

CHAPTER ELEVEN

Rare Hidden Diamonds in Wounded Butterfly Cocoons

by Vanessa Wray

"You must not let your life run in the ordinary way; do something that nobody else has done, something that will dazzle the world. Show that God's creative principle works in you."

~ Paramahansa Yogananda

If before my birth I was warned that I'd lose a parent during my infancy, that the first half of my life would be one heartbreaking obstacle after another, and that one day I'd lose all my blood but miraculously survive, I probably would've chosen a different body to be born into.

For most of my life, there was an image of myself that I held deep inside. It was the image of a lost little girl, incapable of finding her way to the adult world. While I handled the adult responsibilities of a job, bills, and so forth, I was an imposter—a child in an adult's body.

It was a debilitating and grueling feeling, that feeling of being empty and shipwrecked.

It's as if my wheels were forever stuck in mud. No matter how hard I tried to move forward, my wheels just spun furiously. So what made me feel so incapable and powerless to change my life? This is the story of how I got stuck, but also, the story of how I set myself free and learned to grow and thrive, despite so many obstacles.

"Born with a silver spoon" goes the phrase for the rich. I get the feeling I was born stumbling into life, definitely without a silver spoon. Like an uncontrollable tornado, my life spun quickly into wreckage during the first few years of childhood.

When I was an infant, my mother left my biological father, so I never met him. Wanting a better life for us, my mom left our country for the U.S. when I was three, leaving me to live with an uncle. I didn't see her again until I was six, which meant that I spent my most important formative years without either of my parents.

While my uncle provided a comfortable environment, I endured one of my most traumatic experiences while my mother was away. At the hands of a family friend, I fell prey to childhood sexual abuse as early as three or four years old. It continued until I finally was reunited with my mom in the U.S. It could have continued longer if I hadn't moved. I'm so grateful my mom sent for me when she did.

If that wasn't enough to overcome, I fell victim to abuse and harassment again in grade school, in unrelated instances with different people. I was warned never to report it, so no one was aware that these terrible things happened. I did not have the support to tell anyone what was happening, and predators are good at convincing little girls not to tattle. I kept quiet and suffered alone.

The author Jonathan Swift supposedly created the name Vanessa, which was later used to name a type of butterfly. My most influential mentor once asked me, "When will you come out of your cocoon to become the butterfly that you are?" It seemed like an unreachable moment, the time I'd finally burst from a very painfully wound cocoon. I strived yet always felt bound. The abuse was just part of what kept me bound in that cocoon.

When the childhood abuse was over, I still faced numerous, towering obstacles. I had a troubled relationship with my mother, and her relationship with my new stepfather was equally rocky. I retreated into my own world, becoming a serious, introverted recluse. "She's *too* quiet," people would say. Some took it as a sign of calm and control, but inside, I was the twisting storm. I just never felt safe enough to let anyone know what was happening inside me.

Severe depression came early on. I was continuously shuttled between countries to my mother and uncle's homes. Nothing was stable. High school was a battle, and I engaged in reckless, destructive behavior. I abused alcohol, and I often had feelings of not wanting to live. While friends planned for college, I stayed behind. I thought of being an artist— or maybe an architect or psychologist— but my inner world was perpetually dark.

However, even with my constant black cloud looming, one lucky stumble in my teens led me to discover the power of meditation. I read about great spiritual teachers and their philosophies, and I began to meditate on my own. Despite my conflict, this secret practice was calming. But since I battled endless emotions, it took long, arduous years of struggle before I could emerge from the cocoon and truly live.

My first steps into adulthood were a constant struggle. There was never any direction and I often froze with stifling indecisiveness. Relationships faltered, and I made horrible decisions in both school and work. For years I was in and out of college, and any project I started failed. During high points, I opened two small food businesses and ran art workshops. But from those successes, I always fell back into my hole of depression, throwing away whatever progress I made because I felt completely lost.

Once, while with my uncle in my early twenties, I left for a solo-backpacking trip, on a whim without telling anyone. I disappeared quietly and my family frantically searched for me for a month, until I returned home to their relief. Where I'm from, it's not safe for women to travel alone. To me, that trip and other impulsive behaviors were triggered by a constant urge to escape—to be so lost that I could maybe find my way to a new place, some place where I belonged. Maybe a place I would never come back from.

My uncle couldn't understand me at all. How could I invest so much in a business and my studies and then disappear for long stretches after having tasted success?

As my first real father figure, he was an enormous influence on me. When I was born, my family was impoverished. During their childhood, some relatives sold cigarettes on the street for money or they stole neighbors' shirts from the clothesline to "borrow" for school, secretly returning them after school was out. With nothing to his name, my uncle started out sweeping floors for spare change. Many years passed, and he became one of our country's most influential men in his field.

He gave me sage advice, teaching me (by example) lessons about life, work, business, and religion. He was a shining example; he was the most successful person I knew. I was expected to follow in his footsteps and he gave me more than enough support. "You want to study art?" he asked. "Go for it!

"It's business now, you say? Okay. I'll support you in that, too."

But I could never decide what I wanted; partying was more alluring than work. Eventually his frustrated questions became, "Why can't you make up your mind? Why do you keep failing?" The happy, successful life sounded nice, but my mind and heart were too clouded.

Of course, no one knew of my deep depression or experiences. They just saw this lost girl constantly failing. Any light hinting at success quickly grew dim, and I would be back at square one, depressed and more scared than before.

Somewhere along the way though, I was blessed with an introduction to an important spiritual teacher that led me deeper into meditation. He was the same person who asked me when I was scheduled to unveil myself as a "butterfly." With his help, I started leaving my heavy baggage behind. He taught me that I could have full control of my mind and my destiny, an idea that never occurred to me since I was buried in self-pity.

Then eventually, one day I decided I was done with being so utterly sad. That was the day I decided to try "flipping the switch."

Over the years, I learned to manage my turbulent emotions and adjusted to the idea of creating a better life, despite battling my ongoing feelings of being helplessly lost. I purposefully gravitated towards positive people and moved away from the negative, cultivating gratitude for my many blessings. I embraced my new ideals and the successful future I was just beginning to believe was possible.

I looked to inspirational figures that survived horrible hardships. People like Mandela and Gandhi; a blind friend who traversed the city alone and managed a business; the brave girl, Malala Yousafzai; and, of course, my family. These people overcame terrifying hurdles, and I wanted to learn how they found peace and success.

I later experienced some quiet years in my early thirties. However, life brought more upheavals, as it often does. Thinking I was done with feeling anguished, the births of my children interrupted my peaceful new existence. When my son was two days old, he had a stroke and seizures, causing severe brain damage. The doctors grimly predicted he'd have problems walking or talking normally, and could face a difficult life.

Miraculously though, my son defied those predictions. Over the years, he mostly developed like a normal boy, save for some developmental difficulties and a sensory condition. Despite his bleak diagnosis, he turned out dramatically healthier and became my victorious wonder boy!

Then, a few years later, my daughter's delivery also gave way to complications. It was said that this time, I might not survive the birth. "We're doing what we can," the surgeon admitted while I was minutes from dying. After hours of surgery, I somehow managed to survive the ordeal and emerged with my *entire* blood volume replaced with donor blood! Talk about lucky.

Months passed and still more complications arose. A large blood clot formed in my arm where they transfused the blood and caused a serious infection. It took a year and half to recover from childbirth and the complications. I struggled to take care of my newborn daughter and young son since I was weak and sick. I was frail and thin — both mentally and physically exhausted.

Devastated, depression came knocking again; I was worn out from the many agonizing experiences. But because I had been meditating for many years, I managed to recover sooner. Luckily, supportive friends and family helped chase my melancholy away, and as I slowly recovered, a new fire quietly grew inside me. Soon I felt like living again! I was lucky to be alive, and ironically, facing death has always forced me to recognize that I have an amazing life ahead.

After years of struggling for purpose, I suddenly wanted to live like each day was a tremendous gift. I always believed deep down that life is too short to be mediocre, but my sadness kept me from living that belief. I still get the blues occasionally, but the tough times are no longer so low and I can now bounce back and smile. I'm positive and more in control.

Today, with strength renewed, I work as a Health Educator teaching stress management to low-income families (because I know a lot about stress!) I'm delving into writing and digital publishing, and have my sights set on more exciting ventures. Misery is no longer my company. Instead I enjoy time with my kids, dabble in musical and artistic hobbies, and wake up thankful that I'm here and can pursue my dreams.

One vision that keeps me going is something that I feel is part of my bigger purpose. My uncle and mother create and support different projects for underprivileged children—projects such as temporary homes where poor, terminally ill children can stay while they receive medical care. I'm really excited to do similar work, and I'm eagerly building towards this goal.

In the past, I assumed life held some sort of grudge against me. With so many hardships, it was easy to wallow in self-pity. But interestingly, what I really needed was to listen deeply to what these experiences were saying, a profound sharing of so many more truths than I could hope for.

So what's to be learned from darkness and defeat? There's really too much to mention here, but one important point is to find the lesson in each failure. Every downfall has a greater wisdom or power to be gained from it; all darkness contains within it a sliver of light. The deeper you fall, the higher you can bounce upwards. Regardless of the suffering you endure, you can come out of the ashes infinitely stronger and wiser, thanks to your times of weakness.

Secondly, our past failures or circumstances do not have to rule us. To overcome past failures, you must forgive others and yourself, and refuse to let the past control your current life decisions. If you suffered greatly, remember that in the end, everyone is really just searching for love. When someone inflicts pain on others, it could be that they themselves had unmet needs for love, maybe in their childhood. This perspective can enable you to forgive and move forward.

Another practice is fostering gratitude, which helps develop joy. We learn from the past but we also must let go of the negative thoughts and fears of that past. Fears block us from seeing our natural potential to be abundant and joyful people. When you focus on the blessings to be grateful for today, you can let go of fear and regrets from the past.

Also, know in your heart that you have the power to take control of every moment and make it what you want it to be. We can live in despair, or we can shoot for the stars. It seems easier said than done and maybe oversimplified, and I know some circumstances are more debilitating than others. But eventually, you have to just make the decision to pull yourself out of the depths and find a way no matter how difficult it seems, even if you are in the darkest pain.

Most importantly, share your love with others, even if it's just a smile for a stranger. The greater the love you share, the smaller your problems become. Everyone is a butterfly sleeping in a cocoon. Love coaxes timid butterflies out so they can reveal their beautiful potential, like diamonds coming out of the rough.

So, when will you break out of your cocoon? Soon, I hope!

ABOUT THE AUTHOR

A love of healthy living and helping others find lasting health is what guides **Vanessa Wray's** work in public health. Having overcome childhood trauma and deep depression through the use of meditation, she's also passionate about sharing the benefits of meditation for mind, body, and a balanced life. Some of her current endeavors are facilitating stress relief workshops with low-income families and writing about health and the environment on her various websites. On most days you might find her being silly with her children, exploring nature, or dabbling in music and art, outside of work.

Find her at **www.vshanti.com** or **www.healthywonderfoods.com**.

CHAPTER TWELVE

Passion, Perseverance, Resilience: Alex Zanardi, a Champion
by Albina Gabellini

"Start by doing what is necessary, then what is possible, and suddenly you are doing the impossible."

~ **Francis of Assisi**

Alex Zanardi of Bologna, Italy, started his journey in the small town of Castel Maggiore. While his childhood in that historic countryside was charmed, he would first experience tragedy as a teenager, and later, as an adult. These trials would serve to build his character, and eventually, lead to victory.

The first traumatic event struck just a few weeks before Alex's thirteenth birthday, when his older sister went out for ice cream with her fiancé and never returned. Both were killed in an auto crash. Alex and his parents were, naturally, devastated, but this initial tragic experience set the course for the rest of Alex's life.

Not only were his parents grieving the loss of their daughter, but they were also worried about their only son. In another year, Alex would be eligible to drive motorbikes. He was the "wild one" of the family. As could be expected, they feared for his safety.

Fate stepped in. Just before Alex's fourteenth birthday, his father went to visit an old friend at his motorcycle shop. The friend was helping a boy clean his go-kart and, knowing of Alex's father's concern about Alex driving, urged him to buy Alex a go-kart and get him into racing. He said, "Better for your son to burn his desire for speed on a closed circuit than out on the street on a motorcycle."

It worked! Alex loved the go-kart. Instantaneously, he was addicted to racing.

The family was of modest means, so money was often in short supply. Because of this, Alex and his father performed their own modifications and repairs on the go-kart. In doing this, Alex learned about cars from the ground up. He and his father strategized and worked together as Alex gained experience in the world of go-kart racing, reinforcing their relationship and preparing Alex for true competition.

By the end of 1987, Alex had won three Italian go-kart titles and the European championship. At this point, he was ready for bigger and faster cars. He made his professional racing debut in 1988 by joining the Italian Formula 3 series, and by 1990 he had become a serious contender. He then moved up to Formula 3000 Racing, which at that time was equivalent to Formula 1 Racing.

He scored a win in his first Formula 3000 race and followed that up with two more wins that season. His success drew the attention of Formula 1 race teams. Alex made the jump to the big leagues.

However, the next four years were filled with disappointment, as Alex only managed to score a single point. Some of his troubles stemmed from injuries. Perhaps he just never had the right car or team. To make matters worse, the Lotus Team that he was driving for went belly up and he was unable to find another race seat for the 1995 season. His Formula 1 career was over—at least for the time being.

Alex had also suffered another loss, this one much more significant. His beloved father, who had supported him in go-kart racing, passed away in late 1994 after struggling with a serious disease. Alex was devastated.

Since he couldn't find a "ride" in the European Race Circuit, Alex headed to the U.S. with the hope of finding one there.

Alex struggled to find a ride in the U.S. and considered returning home to Italy. Then he was introduced to Chip Ganassi by Rick Gorne, who had witnessed Alex's talent on the Formula 3000 circuit.

Chip Ganassi owned Chip Ganassi Racing that raced in the open-wheel racing category called CART (Championship Auto Racing Teams). Chip gave Alex a test drive, and after turning in a very impressive performance he was signed to the team.

In 1996, his rookie year, Alex won three CART races and was named Champ-Car Rookie of the Year.

Some drivers would be satisfied with that accomplishment, but not Alex! In the last race of the year, in second place, and with only one lap remaining, he once again showed his character. There was only one way he'd be able to win the race, and that would be to pass on a dangerous turn called the Corkscrew. No rational person would pass on that turn, but Alex had never been a "rational" racer. He took the risk and it worked! He passed the competition and won the race. The Corkscrew maneuver he used is so risky that track officials have since banned it.

Alex came back the next season even stronger and won the 1997 CART Championship, competing against Indy Car racing greats such as Michael Andretti, Paul Tracy, and Greg Moore. Alex had hit his stride as a professional racecar driver.

His daring style and charm made him a favorite with both fans and the sports media. The fans liked his post-win antics, such as when he performed victory doughnuts on the track. His attention-getting style even earned him a guest spot on the David Letterman show.

He continued his success the next year by winning the 1998 CART Championship, making him one of only a few to win back-to-back CART Championships. By the end of his time in CART racing, he had won 15 of 66 races and reached the podium 28 times, plus had won two CART Championships.

Alex was on top of the world—a long way from his small hometown in Italy and his first go-kart. He had everything a man could want: a beautiful wife, a baby son, great friends, a house in Monaco, and more. A truly great lifestyle—after all he was achieving this success while doing something he really loved—racing.

His success in CART racing did not go unnoticed. Sir Frank Williams, legendary Formula 1 team owner, offered him a reported $15M contract to race for him.

Maybe it was the lure of bigger paydays.

Maybe he just wanted to crack that Formula 1 nut once and forever.

Maybe it was for the prestige of driving in the world's number one motorsport.

Whatever his reasons were, Alex returned to Formula 1 racing in 1999.

Alex had visions of doing a lot of post-win doughnuts after his Formula 1 wins, but his visions would soon fade. He drove well in the pre-season testing, but everything went downhill from there.

His races were plagued with mechanical failures, crucial mistakes of his own doing and just plain-ole-bad-luck. The season ended without Alex scoring a single point. He was dropped from the team, leaving him to spend the year of 2000 in reflection.

Alex contacted his former CART team. Fortunately, they were happy to have him rejoin.

In 2001, Alex was scheduled to race in Lausitzring, Germany. The race was one of only a few CART races held outside the U.S. and was almost called off because of the horrific 9/11 terrorist attacks in New York City. However, after talking to the teams and drivers, the race promoters decided to go ahead with the race and renamed it the American Memorial 500.

Maybe it was because the race was being run in honor of the 9/11 victims in his adopted homeland, or maybe he just found his groove again, but whatever the reason, Alex raced like a man on a mission.

He was holding a commanding lead with only 13 laps remaining when he was called in for his final pit stop. That's when tragedy struck. His life would never be the same again.

That is, if he even lived through the day.

It's still a mystery as to what exactly happened when he exited the pit area. Some speculate that he hit an oil slick on his way back onto the track. Some think he hit some wet grass on the edge of the track.

But whatever the cause of the skid, the fact was that his car ended up in the middle of the racing lane, broadside to the oncoming cars.

He was a sitting duck and cars were racing towards him at nearly 200 miles per hour. The first car to reach him was able to swerve around him, but the second car, driven by Alex Tagliani, was not so lucky.

The nose of Tagliani's racecar hit Zanardi's car just in front of the cockpit. The impact blasted car parts up to 200 yards away. The front of the chassis, along with Alex's legs, went one direction. The cockpit and the rear of the car, along with Alex's torso, went a different direction.

CART's emergency team, led by Dr. Terry Trammel, raced towards the shattered car knowing that they probably only had about three minutes to save Alex's life. As the team neared the car, Dr. Trammel slipped in what he initially thought was a pool of oil but later realized was Alex's blood. Blood spewed from the veins and arteries in both of Alex's amputated legs. The doctor had to think fast. In a matter of minutes, Alex would bleed out.

The doctor stuck his fingers in the veins and arteries that were bleeding the worst until the emergency crew could fashion belts into tourniquets. They slowed the bleeding enough to extract Alex from the car and get him to the helicopter waiting to take him to the hospital.

The racetrack chaplain administered Last Rites to Alex before the chopper lifted off. He had seen drivers pass from this life before and was sure Alex would not make it.

Alex's life hung by a very thin thread. His heart stopped multiple times on the 37-minute flight to Berlin and had to be restarted each time with heart massage.

By the time he reached the hospital, Alex had less than a liter of blood remaining. He was rushed into an eight-hour emergency surgery where the doctors worked feverishly to save his life and as much of his legs as they could.

After doing all they could, the doctors put Alex in a medically induced coma and hoped for the best. They would not know until they brought him out of the coma three days later if he had suffered permanent brain damage.

The doctors decided that Alex's wife should be the one to tell him that he had lost his legs in the accident. She was at his bedside when he was brought out of the coma. She delivered the news and then reassured him that she was going to stand by him, no matter what, and that he would walk again someday.

Alex listened quietly to her and then assured her that they would "find a way through this." Then he said, "Now let me go back to sleep. I'm tired." His reaction to what most people would consider disastrous news was so typical of him. His first instinct was to think about possibilities rather than about what he could no longer do or had lost.

Hearing this much, you would probably assume that Alex would never race again. Wrong!

In 2003, Alex was invited to come back to the track where he had lost his legs and finish the 13 laps that he didn't get a chance to finish. But if anyone thought that he came back to just ceremonially finish the laps, they were mistaken. He wanted to see if he could still compete. He lapped the track with a specially modified car at speeds up to 186 miles per hour. Fast enough that had he been qualifying for the race that weekend, he would have been fifth in the starting polls.

His racing career was not over yet. BMW modified a 320i and signed him to a contract to regularly race in the World Touring Car Championship (WTCC). Between 2004 and 2009, he racked up five wins and five podiums—not too shabby for someone most people thought would never race again.

Alex branched out into other competitive arenas as well. In 2007, he got involved in paracycling (aka hand-cycling) partially to get himself in better shape and partially for the competition. In 2011, he won the Paracycling Class of the New York Marathon, and in 2012, he won two gold medals at the London Paralympics.

The man refused to be limited.

In October of 2014, Alex competed in his first ever Ironman triathlon and finished the competition 272nd out of 2,187 participants with a time of 9 hours, 47 minutes, 14 seconds. One year later, he competed in the grueling competition again—besting his time by 7 minutes and finishing 167th out of 2,425 participants.

Alex has always lived his life with passion, persistence, and resilience. Undoubtedly those character traits have kept him going when most people would simply quit. As a result, he has bounced back from many setbacks, defeats, and failures.

When a reporter asked him what was next in his life, Alex replied, "I have to tell you that the possibilities are not lacking in my life, and this is something for which I feel very lucky."

Alex's life truly personifies the saying that "failure is never final, unless you decide that it is."

Don't expect Alex's story to end like some stories—with the hero riding off into the sunset. Not anytime soon anyway—and probably not unless he's driving his specially modified BMW off into the sunset—at about 200 miles per hour!

ABOUT THE AUTHOR

Albina Gabellini is an Italy-based researcher, entrepreneur, coach and pedagogue. She holds multiple degrees and certificates, including a master's degree in education and a bachelor's degree in economics and business.

She had a successful career with ITT and Control Data Corporation, where she helped develop the first distance learning programs.

A highly sought business coach for more than 40 years, she is also the author of *Cognitive Coaching*.

Albina has done significant scientific research in the field of "resilience," the human capacity to adapt to the challenges of life. The Resilient method serves to reinforce in people all the skills capable of dealing with problems, such as bereavement, loss, failure, abandonment, humiliation and betrayal.

She is the mother of two, grandmother of one and aunt of six nieces, while maintaining an active career as a researcher, entrepreneur, coach and pedagogue.

She can be contacted at **www.bettercoaching.it** and **info@gsm-online.it**

CHAPTER THIRTEEN

The Courage to Continue
by Thomas Robert Hutcherson

"Success consists of going from failure to failure without loss of enthusiasm."

~ Sir Winston Churchill

The year was 1993. I was 25 years old, living back at home with my parents in a small two-bedroom apartment. I did not have a job, and I was strapped with more consumer debt than I had imagined possible.

A couple of years earlier I had achieved what I considered to be a significant level of success. How had I sunk to these new lows? And how would I climb back out of this hole to find success and fulfillment again? I had to discover the five principles I now use to guide my life. Once I learned, and decided to implement those principles into my life, I became successful again. I now live my life day by day by these core principles.

Three years before my low point, while still in college at the University of South Carolina, I launched a computer business with a friend of mine. I enjoyed the work immensely. It gave me a feeling of satisfaction. I was making what I thought was good money at the time. It seemed to be the perfect situation! After all, I didn't have a boss telling me what to do, I was living life on my terms, and I was enjoying the personal and business relationships that were being established along the way. Life was good on all accounts.

Our company, aptly named "Personal Business Systems," even had its own fancy logo placed on all of the computers that we custom built, sold, and delivered. Upon graduation from college, we were rocking and rolling along when, out of the blue, my business partner announced that he had decided to take a job in Florida. As such, he wanted to cash out all of his interest. Looking back on it now, I am not sure why I was so devastated, except the fact that I no longer had anyone helping me with the management of finances. It just wasn't the same endeavor without my friend and business partner. It probably was the first time I felt truly alone or on my own.

Luckily, one of our largest accounts, East Educational Services (EES), had a bid out for 200 computer systems and four local area networks—each with its own file server. This was the largest order to date, with well over $30,000 in net profit projected. Mr. Ken East, the company founder and owner expressed concerns about awarding the job to my company without my business partner involved. Subsequently, he offered me a salaried position within his organization, which included all the typical benefits—health insurance, paid vacation, sick days, and, of course, a nice steady paycheck. It seemed like a win-win all around, as not only did it allow for the large order to progress, but also it enabled me to move into a more secure position.

The amount of profit from this one project alone would more than pay a year of my salary—$28,000. That seemed like a lot of money to a young man not long out of college back in the early 90s. However, something very interesting happened to me. Once I went to work in a full time position, the days seemed to get much longer. I no longer had much control of my days or of my time. I felt like a round peg being jammed into a square hole. I told myself that I had to stick it out for a full year. After all, I felt that I owed my new employer at least that much. I was working hard to establish a new computer hardware division within his company. I wanted to do the best I could for him and the rest of the people that worked there.

After a year had passed, I realized that I had given up something very important. I was far happier as a business owner than as a salaried employee. My happiness was worth a price. Additionally, I felt that my life was no longer going in a good direction. I had the stability of a salaried job, but I felt empty inside. I was at a major roadblock. I couldn't just go back into business on my own again, or could I? Would that even make me feel happy or fulfilled?

About the same time, one of my best friend's aunt, who happened to be living in Austin, Texas, had told me how terrific it was to be living there. I figured it would be worth looking into while visiting my parents, since Austin, just north from where my parents had now retired, was only a few hours away from them. I flew out to visit my folks using the vacation time I had earned. What had been reported I found to be very true. To my delight, everywhere I went, the people in Texas were indeed very friendly and nice. I knew right away that this might be a good move for me to make. My parents encouraged me to move to Texas, even if it was only to stay with them at first. After all, I was still a young single man, only in my mid-twenties. I decided it was a done deal. I would move in with my folks for a short time with the ultimate goal to subsequently re-establish myself with a new life.

Now that I had decided to move, I struggled with the process of giving my two-week notice. I worried about what my boss would think, if the news would be taken well, and if my choice would affect my future negatively. Amazingly, once I did give my notice, I felt huge relief, like a large weight had been lifted. The plan was now in action; a new adventure now awaited me in Texas. To make things even better, the company president gave me the name and number to a local businessman, Mr. Dale DeStefano, telling me to give him a call once I got settled. This ended up being a great stepping-stone job that helped me get back on my feet. In retrospect, providing this contact information, which landed me my new job in Texas, was a very nice thing and much appreciated to this day. Looking back, I am very thankful to Ken, Irv, and to all the many good people that I had worked with at EES, my first real job out of college.

Once I was moved and situated, I gave Mr. DeStefano a call. We negotiated a rather low hourly pay. Considering my qualifications, he got one terrific deal, but not being currently employed and with no connections, I did not have much negotiation power. I was, however, eager to get back to work.

Plus I was making new friends. One guy in particular named Randy, who lived in the same apartment complex as my parents, became a good buddy of mine. He just so happened to know some people living in Austin, which was a few hundred miles away. It wasn't long before we were driving up to Austin for weekends. I did computer work during the days and helped my dad on the weekends building houses. The only problem with helping my dad was, just like when I was living at home growing up (or at any time since) there was never any pay involved. Any work I did for him did not count toward paying my bills and I was in need of income—in a big way.

Now in my mid-twenties, my financial day of reckoning had arrived. It was apparent that I had made quite a large financial mess of my affairs. I was carrying large debts on credit cards, plus my student loans were also due, adding to the amount of money I was paying out on a regular basis. While in college, I had accumulated what now felt like an insurmountable amount of debt since I had used credit cards and student loans to enjoy the lifestyle that I had so desired. Since then, my debt had snowballed. The job I now had in Corpus Christi at DD Computer Warehouse paid much less than my full-time salaried job that I had before at EES. I could no longer pay my bills, even while living rent-free with my parents.

As it turned out, through my new connections that I had made through my friend Randy, I was able to land a terrific engineering job with a $35,000 annual salary and full benefits. And where was this job? In Austin, of course, where I ultimately wanted to live! After two weeks of on-the-job training with one of the senior engineers, Mr. Gerald Richard, I was flying solo doing field engineering work. It was very challenging work in the environmental field, but I worked hard to do my best. As a result, I began tackling my debt problem while finding satisfaction in my career and life overall.

Not long after that, I met the lady of my dreams—a very nice, soft-spoken Asian woman by the name of JoJo. She is such a special lady in so many ways. We started spending most of our waking hours together, attending social activities and going to the movies. After dating for three to four months and a yearlong engagement, we celebrated a whirlwind of a wedding filled with much joy, friends, and family.

JoJo changed my life by being a fabulous partner. Our life together has not been without struggle. We have our ups and downs like any marriage has, but I think we have the commitment that makes a marriage successful—the willingness and desire to work through life's struggles together. Today, we are blessed with two sons. I can only hope that each of our sons will one day find wives that are as terrific as their mother.

JoJo and I have lived important principles that I now realize my parents first modeled for me. My mother worked very hard—going to work early every day and on weekends working in the family business alongside my father. She also introduced me to church at an early age. My father introduced me to the world of business. I am very thankful to the both of them, as they have continued to demonstrate their commitment to each other through the struggles they have faced together, recently celebrating 50 years of marriage. JoJo and I now walk in faith as we work to provide a stable home for ourselves and our two sons.

To summarize, the principles I found, that I had previously mentioned earlier, are: Expectations, Goals, Responsibility, Discipline, and Thankfulness, or (EGRD&T for short).

These five principles are the most important of any that I have learned. First, have expectations in the outcomes that you seek, in the people with whom you interact, and generally in how you expect life to work for you. When you do this, you are setting yourself up to find the results that you desire from the start.

Second, set written goals, both personal and professional. Without goals, you are like a ship on the high seas without a rudder. Where will you end up? It's anyone's guess. If you don't have goals, your life will always be adrift. For starters, if you think you are "too busy," start each day with the most important three goals you have for the day. Each day repeat this process, striking out what you have accomplished and adding new goals. You will likely find yourself pleasantly surprised at your new accomplishments!

Want to rid yourself of all your consumer debt? Consumer debt is the largest burden on our society and will likely destroy our nation, if the damage has not been done already, what with a mounting national deficit in the trillions of dollars. Make it your goal to be debt-free in two to five years. You can do it. There are a ton of resources available, but first you must make it your goal and a priority in your life. Take charge!

Third, take personal responsibility for your life. Until you accept the fact that you are in charge of your life, you are setting yourself up for failure. Personal responsibility is being responsible for your actions. Want to lose weight? Educate yourself on proper portion size, diet, and exercise. You can do it, but you must learn to be more responsible for your behaviors if you wish to succeed. Don't go it alone; seek out the help you need, as behavior change is exceptionally challenging to accomplish.

Fourth, you must have discipline, the discipline to control how you act and behave, to get up each morning, and to make the best of each day. This is the key to everything you do; it all starts with your attitude! You want better results in your life? Start your day with a positive mental attitude.

To build discipline, I would suggest enrolling in a Taekwondo class, getting involved at the local YMCA, or seeking out a good church in your community so you can become involved as a volunteer over time. Better yet, do all three if you can! With discipline, you can likely accomplish most any goal you set for yourself—personally or professionally.

And finally, you need to cultivate thankfulness in your life as a habit. Life is short and fleeting. What do you have in your life to be thankful for? Learn to give thanks each day for what life brings you. Your health, family, and friends—all the important things that make life worth living!

Don't like where your life is right now? Feeling like a failure? Not sure how to get motivated? Start today to cultivate new habits to transform your life by implementing the five principles that I found are most important: Expectations, Goals, Responsibility, Discipline, and Thankfulness (EGRD&T) into your life, and over time, you will make terrific strides with positive transformation to improve your life. You can go from failure to success by working these five principles into your daily habits. Make it your goal to give it a go at least 40 days, then reflect on how you are doing. May you find much joy, happiness, and success as you put in place EGRD&T into your life habits.

ABOUT THE AUTHOR

Thomas Robert Hutcherson was born May 2, 1968 in the small rural town of Elizabethtown, Kentucky. Etown, as it is more commonly known by the local town folk, is just 10.5 miles from Hodgenville, KY (which you may be surprised to learn is the birthplace of President Abraham Lincoln).

When Thomas was a child, his family traded in the cold, snowy farming lifestyle, moving from a 117-acre Kentucky farm to the warmer coastal climate of Corpus Christi, Texas, aka "the Sparkling City by the Sea." Not yet settling down, his family moved again, this time to the sunny South Carolina coast. As a teen, he worked after school in the family-owned import business.

After graduating from Beaufort Academy in 1986, he attended the University of South Carolina, earning a Bachelor of Science degree in computer science in 1991. From there he went on to work in the computer industry, setting up networking and hardware divisions for several small companies. In 1993 he moved west where he now resides in Austin, Texas with his wife and two sons. Professionally, he is currently working on building a successful insurance agency. Additionally, he is a licensed Texas Realtor® since 1995, helping buyers and sellers in their transactions and enjoys investing in the real estate and financial markets.

Please visit **http://www.thomasrhutcherson.com** or via email, **TheCourageToContinue@austin.rr.com** to connect with him.

CHAPTER FOURTEEN

Greek Olympic Athlete Trains Running Barefoot on Rocks to Feed His Country

by Joan Junker

"Only those who dare to fail greatly can ever achieve greatly."

~Robert F. Kennedy

In 1946, as the rest of Europe was rebuilding, Greece was still torn apart by civil war. In Athens, lines for soup kitchens remained. People were dying of starvation. Greeks struggled just to survive, living on the little food they could get from ration cards, gardens, or trades with neighbors. Jewelry was bartered for olive oil, butter, or sugar.

However, out of this crisis a great Greek Olympian arose—Stylianos (Stelios) Kyriakides—a man who took heroic action to help the world understand the plight of the Greek people.

123

Kyriakides was fortunate enough to have a job. He worked as a bill collector for the utility company, but was heartsick as he watched parents foregoing rations in order to feed their children, and even worse, homeless children fending for themselves on the streets.

Through all this, he continued to slowly walk his collection route in hopes of renewing some impression of a normal life. While working his route, customers who remembered his running and what it had done for Greece would occasionally give him potatoes and lettuce.

Kyriakides wanted his family to remain intact. Having survived near execution and hunger, which many friends and fellow Olympic athletes were unable to escape, it appeared his running career was finished. He was thirty-five and had not competed in five years.

Worn, frail, and emaciated, he intensified his focus on his family and country. He humbled himself, attending church regularly and observing all of the holidays. He spent time with his family, listening to music and the radio.

His wife, Iphigenia, observed his obvious depression, but she assumed he was not able to run due to the mental and physical toll the war had taken on him. It was all he could do to stay alive and keep his family fed.

Many Greeks wondered how much longer they could last. When would the struggle end?

Because there was no fighting in Cyprus, Stylianos decided to return to his birthplace with his wife and children. During this time, the British government was helping Cypriots reunite with their families by covering their costs, so he and his family could afford to make this move.

Once there, they were quarantined in an army base with thousands of others for 40 days. They were given food to eat, and Kyriakides started running barefoot along the beaches of Cyprus. The sand helped him regain the strength in his legs.

While running, he remembered the horrible night in Halandri when he was almost executed. He decided he had been spared for a reason and began searching for a way to save his country.

He approached his wife with his idea as they waited out the quarantine period. Tentatively, he shared the premonition he had. Then he told her he was going to America to win the marathon for Greece. After the quarantine, with the support of a temporary job, he moved his family where many relatives could help them. He restarted his training and worked out in a gym. Sadly, no matter how hard he worked, he was unable to regain the weight or strength of his prewar condition.

In September, he returned to his job with the utility company, which offered a better future and some benefits. Greece was still in turmoil and struggling to return to some sense of normal. Road infrastructure was still in ruins, transportation was at a standstill, and the countryside was no longer producing the foods it had previously.

As he walked his route, he saw the children searching the streets for food and adults collapsing from starvation. It was too much; the desire to return to Boston became much stronger. He approached Iphigenia again to tell her his desire to run the marathon. He felt that if he went to Boston and won, the world would gain awareness of what was happening in Greece and aid would follow. His wife, however, was very worried that she would lose him to running, especially since he barely had survived the war.

After much assurance and the promise to train with Otto Simitsek (his coach from previous Balkan Games, the Olympics, and the 1938 Boston Marathon), she agreed to let him go. The race was in less than four months. They realized they might have to sell some things, including the radio and stove. His wife knew how much he enjoyed listening to the radio and teased him that she did not mind selling the radio, but she could not part with her stove. He promised her he would buy a new stove for her when he came back from Boston as the winner.

The next day he spoke with Leslie Kemp, his boss who had always backed him before. Kemp saw how much Kyriakides' health had declined since 1938 and wondered why he wanted to go back to Boston. Kyriakides told him he had seen what the war had done to the people of Greece and wanted to help. Running was what he could do. Kemp agreed to pay for his expenses.

Kyriakides was determined not to repeat his experience at the 1938 Boston Marathon. This time he would win.

In 1938, after running in the Berlin Olympics, the Greek-Americans in Boston were excited to have a Greek race in their marathon. They helped him get to America where he was treated like royalty. Jerry Nason of the Boston Globe took a liking to him and sensed a champion behind his quiet demeanor.

The morning of the run, Kyriakides decided to race in new running shoes on harder pavement than he was used to in Greece. About ten miles into the race, he felt blisters forming. After running a bit more, he stopped to remove his shoe and tried to make an adjustment. He saw the pack running away so he hurriedly put his shoe back on and started running. His feet were bleeding and he was favoring his injured foot.

Over the next eight miles he lost valuable time. The heat sapped him. Sweat poured into his shoes, irritating the blisters.

Just short of the twenty-one mile mark, Kyriakides saw a passing bus and flagged it down. Embarrassed and in pain, he boarded the bus, which only took him to Lake Street. After getting off the bus, he looked down to see blood seeping through his shoes. He raised his hand for help, and a car stopped. However, this car was only going as far as Beacon Street, where he had to get out again.

This time he walked into a nearby drugstore. A surprised pharmacist informed him that he was restricted by law and was not able to give him the medicine he needed. He dejectedly walked back out and whistled loudly to stop a passing cab and got a ride to the finish line. Other exhausted, dejected runners had also thumbed rides to the finish line. His friend Johnny Kelly from the 1936 Berlin Games came in third. Tarzan Brown, who had previously won, finished an hour slower than his best time.

Ashamed, he spoke to reporters and congratulated the winner and other racers. He felt he had let down all of Greece and the Greek-Americans who had counted on him. He told Nason that one day he would be back and would maybe win the marathon.

In 1946, after the war and devastation in Greece, Kyriakides had a new purpose for running the Boston Marathon. This time he was going to win, but first he had to get there and train so he could be accepted in the race.

He faced daunting obstacles. He was eight years older and no longer at the peak of his abilities. He had only been training for a few months, hadn't eaten right or stayed in shape, and was concerned about his mental ability to get through the race. To overcome these factors, he trained in the mountains where the terrain was difficult so he could toughen his heart and spirit. He relied on his drive to push him.

He started the same training program that he had used for years, which included stamina and speed workouts. Sometimes Simitsek rode alongside him on a bike or in a car, shouting encouragement and advice. He ran a hundred miles or more per week, sometimes on hard ground or rocks. Later, he started removing his shoes to toughen up his feet. Seeing Kyriakides running was not unusual, but few knew why he was working so hard.

Near the first of April, he began packing his things for the trip. He shared with his family that he may be gone a month or more because he had to go many places to tell everyone that would listen how there was no food for the families in Greece.

On April 2nd, he explained to his in-laws why he was going to Boston. They thought he was crazy and told him that he did not have a chance of winning. He told them they would eat their words at Easter. Because April 19th fell on Good Friday, the race was moved to April 20th. The time difference meant the race would end in Greece late on the night before Easter, so his wife would not know the results until Easter morning. He asked her to listen to the radio at 7:30 a.m. for the results.

The next day he and Simitsek boarded the flight to America. In Boston, on April 8th, Jerry Nason heard a knock on his door. He did not recognize the stranger until Kyriakides smiled. It was then that Nason recognized his friend and the promise that was made eight years earlier. Kyriakides asked Nason to tell the story of the horror and death that had overtaken Greece, not of him as a runner. He shared how some of his Olympic teammates had died due to starvation and lack of medical attention and how he had to sell clothes, shoes, and furniture to keep his family alive.

This would not be a typical feature story about another runner. Greece had no food, no clothing, no roads, no bridges, no harbors—only the land and people determined to survive. When Nason asked Kyriakides if he had enough stamina to run, the response was maybe not in his legs, but he had the strength in his heart.

On the day of the race, several doctors were at the starting line making sure the runners were fit to run. Kyriakides was sitting for the pre-race weigh in when one of the doctors solemnly told him he could not run. His Greek-American sponsor told the doctor that Greece would take the responsibility if anything happened to him during the race. He was allowed to run.

Coming to "Heartbreak Hill," he was running alongside Johnny Kelly. He was very fatigued and worried whether he could win when he heard an old man shout in Greek, "For Greece! For your children!"

Encouraged by the raw emotion in the man's voice, Kyriakides took off. Johnny Kelley later stated that there was no stopping him at that point.

As he cut across the finish line, Kyriakides raised his hands and cried, "For Greece!"

Back in Athens, Iphigenia had been waiting for the news. She was sitting in the chair holding their son when the BBC announcer delivered the news that a Greek, Stylianos Kyriakides, had won the 50th Boston Marathon. She dropped her son, quickly scooped him up again, and ran to tell her parents. At first they could not believe it. Soon neighbors were banging on the door. They also had heard the news!

In the United States, Kyriakides traveled from Boston to Washington to New York to spread the word of the plight of the Greeks. Word traveled, and the response brought over $250,000 in cash, clothing, food, medical equipment, and supplies for his fellow countrymen.

When he returned home, Kyriakides received a king's welcome. Nearly a million people turned out for the parade. After several hours of dignitary stops and speeches, he was back in his home for the first time in over a month.

That evening the Acropolis was lit up for the first time after the war.

He was able to unite a country that was divided by civil war and bring hope to the people. Today both sides fly their Greek flags with pride.

Stylianos Kyriakides learned from his failure at the Boston marathon in 1938. Even though his initial failure was devastating and humiliating, it drove him to be successful in 1946.

For some of you, this may be the first time you have heard of him. Hopefully, you now can see how important he was to the history of Greece. He brought pride back to a nation and removed the look of resignation from their eyes. He used his skills to gain assistance for his countrymen and to end a civil war.

For me the lesson of Kyriakides is: If at first you fail (no matter how devastating), never, never, give up! Try, try again!

ABOUT THE AUTHOR

Joan Junker: My life of 30 plus years of experience in the graphic arts and printing industry, working trade shows and major international events throughout the world, including the Olympics and Paralympics, has allowed me to live and travel around the world learning and living in other cultures.

I currently coach businesses and individuals globally in major event project management, operations, sponsorships, marketing, and other areas.

I enjoy sharing lessons learned and finding a way to make life easier for others.

My hope is for people to focus on what is possible and not let failure stop them. Focus on what can be done and the ultimate goal will be achieved.

Share your successes at email: **joan.junker1@gmail.com**.

A Radical Faith Does Radical Things

by Steve Highsmith

"I am doing a great work, and I can't come down."

~ **Nehemiah 6:3** (NCV)

In the spring of 2012, 13-year-old Lily Shields, a seventh grader, was an up-and-coming long distance track star. Lily ran several events, but her specialty was the 2400-meter, a grueling mile and a half distance that is especially long for middle school girls.

Lily didn't mind; she was fast. So fast that she was already eyeing the school record; her goal was to beat that record the following year as an eighth grader. It looked like she would do it. Her times were steadily decreasing, becoming very competitive with high school records. Lily dreamed of a successful high school cross country career and the college scholarship offers that would follow.

Not only was she fast, but Lily loved running. It was an activity she shared with her father, Jeff. They ran 5K races together every month and spent a great deal of quality time together. It was also an activity that allowed Lily to serve through an organization called ActiveWater, a charity that funds the infrastructure necessary to supply safe drinking water in Africa. Lily and Jeff had raised over $2000 for ActiveWater thus far and wanted to raise much more.

After a successful seventh grade track season, Lily began her last year in middle school. Because her middle school didn't have a cross-country program, she trained with her dad during the fall and winter. All seemed to be going well, until one day in March of 2013, while on a Spring Fling 5K run with her father, Lily experienced extreme pain in her legs and feet.

She finished the race, but the pain didn't go away. She took a break from running, but she still didn't get relief. Lily had x-rays taken but the doctors could not identify what the problem was. She underwent physical therapy, but again, no improvement. The pain was so great that Lily missed the entire eighth grade track season. It was a devastating blow.

The fall brought high school and the beginning of the cross-country season. Lily's therapy hadn't produced any meaningful progress, but she was still hopeful that she would start as a freshman. In September, while on a freshman retreat, Lily suffered a concussion after accidentally being hit on the head with a board. Suddenly Lily had to shift from "feet therapy" to "concussion therapy." Her doctors told her she needed to focus on her brain injury and suspend any running recovery.

Over the next 12 months, with her running career on hold, Lily looked to her other strengths and passions for comfort. She soon discovered there was none to be found. In the winter of her freshman year, she auditioned for the lead in a community theater production, but she didn't get the role. Near the end of her freshman year, she auditioned for her school's top choral group, but she wasn't selected for the choir. In the fall of her sophomore year, she auditioned for the lead in the high school drama. Again, she didn't get the role.

As she was nearing the midpoint of her sophomore year in high school, she received the final dagger. After almost 18 months of x-rays, therapy and continued rest that didn't provide a reprieve from the pain, Lily had an MRI performed on her legs. The test results showed stress fractures in both feet. Her high school running career was officially over before it had even begun.

Lily had sunk into deep despair. She felt worthless as all the activities she loved continued to disappoint her. Her father said, "It was failure after failure after failure. And it wasn't just that she was trying new things that weren't working. She was failing in all the activities she loved and was very good at—running, acting, and singing. It seemed like Lily just couldn't catch a break."

What Lily hadn't realized yet was that, although several doors were closing on the things she had previously loved and excelled at, God was beginning to open her heart to a new passion—the people of Haiti. In the summer of 2013, Lily and her mother, Krista, spent a week on a mission trip with their church hosting a Vacation Bible School for children in Haiti. While on the trip they spent a day at the Wholehearted Orphanage in Fonds Parisien, Haiti, which is 30 miles east of the capital city of Port au Prince and eight miles west of the Dominican Republic border. Wholehearted Orphanage is a ministry of Haitian Christian Mission that provides a safe environment for just a few of the over 750,000 orphans in Haiti. The orphanage currently houses 12 children and two house parents.

The following summer, in July 2014, Lily's entire family, including her sister, Annie, completed a 10-day mission trip to Haiti with their church. On this trip, the family spent part of every day at Wholehearted. During one of these visits, Lily learned of Wholehearted's vision to build a new compound consisting of eight homes, large enough to house 96 children and eight sets of house parents. The cost of the project was estimated at the time to be $1,474,000. Lily was inspired. There were 27 people on her mission team, so Lily decided to take on the responsibility for 1/27th of the cost herself. She set a goal to raise $54,592.59.

When she returned to the United States, Lily announced that, in lieu of any gifts for her 16th birthday in August, she wanted friends and family to contribute to her fundraiser. She made pleas to her church and youth group. The result? Lily raised $13,000 from these contributions (including some generous corporate donations).

In the coming months, she spoke to several youth groups and Girl Scout troops in her community. Using mostly penny jars to collect loose change, she raised $20,000 by the following summer.

In the summer of 2015, as Lily prepared for her third trip to Haiti, she first went on a retreat with her church youth group. While at the conference Lily's heart was moved again by the group's program, "Give Up and Go Be," and she decided to go from just financially supporting the people of Haiti from afar to serving them directly. How would she do this? By becoming a missionary in Haiti. When they visited Haiti for two weeks in July, Lily and her family witnessed work being completed on the new Wholehearted site as the protective foundation wall was being built around the new 3.5 acre compound.

As her 17th birthday drew near in August, Lily decided that she needed an outlandish plan to finally reach her fundraising goal, which was still some $34,000 short. In August 2015, she announced a request that, in honor of her 17th birthday, she dreamed that 2000 people would each donate $17 so she could raise the remaining $34,000 within 30 days. To entice donors to participate, Lily declared that she would shave her head and keep it shaved for 30 days if she was successful. She also convinced three students, a teacher, and the principal of her school to agree to shave their heads if she met incremental goals during the 30 days. Lily really wanted at least one female to join her in her "Wholeheartedly Bald for Haiti" campaign. The night before the kickoff, her sister Annie agreed to participate.

Lily set up a GoFundMe page and created a series of YouTube videos to assist in her fundraising efforts. Over the next couple of weeks, donations began to come in. Her school jumped on the bandwagon, enthusiastically promoting her cause. Friends and family members shared her goals through social media platforms. A few businesses made matching gifts, and as the 30-day deadline approached, the goal was in sight. On the morning of the 30th day, Lily was still short of the goal by over $3000, but just after 8:00 that evening, the total surpassed $34,000. Lily had met her goal!

Lily and Annie both shaved their heads in celebration. Of course, Lily fulfilled her pledge to keep her head shaved for thirty days. During this time, Lily was inducted into her school's chapter of the National Honor Society and was also named to the homecoming court at school. Lily appeared on the football field at halftime of the homecoming game wearing a formal evening gown while sporting a bald head!

In January 2016, Lily made her first solo trip to Haiti as she completed a two-week internship with the director of the Wholehearted Orphanage. While there, she learned how Haitian Christian Mission works, how Wholehearted Orphanage operates, and what jobs might be available for her in the future. She also saw firsthand the progress being made at the new compound as the foundation wall was nearing completion and final plans were being made for the first duplex within the wall.

Lily's next outlandish plan is to "Bike to Haiti" in the summer of 2016 in an attempt to raise $86,000 to help build the first duplex in the community. Lily and Jeff, along with eight other riders, plan to bicycle from their home in Indiana to Florida while Krista and Annie follow behind in an RV. Then, after they fly from Florida to Haiti, they intend to bike the remaining 30 miles from Port au Prince to Wholehearted.

The past four years have been an interesting journey for Lily. Just a short time ago, she dreamed of being a star athlete and receiving many college scholarships. Now, she still intends to go to college but she wishes to do so as part of her preparation for a lifetime of mission work in Haiti.

Lily has no regrets. She understands the big picture. She knows that if she had stayed healthy and was still pursuing a running career, she wouldn't have the time or energy for the Wholehearted Orphanage and its financial needs. She has raised almost $60,000 for various causes in her short lifetime and has plans to double that number in just the upcoming year. She has become an inspiration to many students and adults in her community.

Yet through it all, she remains faithful, humble, and soft-spoken. She has lived through high times—running with her dad, giving to others, looking forward to a bright athletic future. She has been through low times—a career-ending injury and a seemingly never-ending string of failures in a very short time. She's back on the high—serving children in Haiti, knowing what she wants in life, and most importantly, knowing what God wants for her life. She is in love with the people of Haiti, she is in love with God, and she can't wait to see what's in store in her future.

It is often said that when God closes one door, He opens another, but it is not always that simple. Most of the time, opportunities present themselves when you aren't really looking for them. You don't always have to hit rock bottom before the upward journey begins again. Lily made her first trip to Haiti over a year before the MRI officially ended her running career and before some of the other failures she experienced. She certainly wasn't looking for something new that would change her life forever, but it appeared anyway. The seed of inspiration was planted before she realized it was the path she would take.

My advice: Keep your eyes open for the opportunities around you. They are there. Always be open to the possibilities that exist for you.

They are unlimited. At all times, but especially when you encounter failure, keep an open mind. You never know what the future holds.

As her father has said, "The things in Lily's life that would bring honor to Lily were ending. The things in her life that would bring honor to God have just begun."

How about you? No matter what you're currently experiencing, there is success out there for you. Go get it!

To learn more about **Lily Shields**, her mission, and her vision, visit: **www.wholeheartedinhaiti.wix.com/site.** To learn more about the Wholehearted Orphanage, visit: **www.wholeheartedorphanage.com.**

ABOUT THE AUTHOR

Steve Highsmith is a Certified Financial Planner™ professional in Brownsburg, IN, a suburb of Indianapolis. He is an independent, fee-only planner, providing advice to people from all walks of life without minimum account requirements, sales commissions, or long-term commitments. He proudly embraces his fiduciary duty, always placing his clients' best interests first.

He has had a passion for personal development since being introduced to Jim Rohn in 2001. He considers Jim Rohn, Darren Hardy, Vic Johnson, and Brian Tracy to be his biggest mentors.

Steve and his wife Carol live on the west side of Indianapolis with their two beautiful and amazing daughters, Allison and Abby. Contact Steve at **www.SteveHighsmith.com.**

CHAPTER SIXTEEN

I Brought the Monster to Its Knees
by Doug Evans

"Failure should be our teacher, not our undertaker. Failure is delay, not defeat. It is a temporary detour, not a dead end. Failure is something we can avoid only by saying nothing, doing nothing, and being nothing."

~ Denis Waitley

This is a story about failure. How you view failure and how I view failure may very well be two totally different things. Most people would say that failure is a lack of success, or some sort of defeat. Some would define it as a non-fulfillment of a goal or dream. Still others would define it as lack of achievement.

I'm about to tell you about failure from the eyes of a little boy. I'll call him Benny. You could call him Joey or Mikey or whatever, but the lesson you're going to learn from this story will be exactly the same.

This is going to sound like it's a golf story, and it is, but more than anything else, it's a story about failure, passion, hope, perseverance, and long-awaited success. It's a story about people that have the cards stacked against them—people who are up against daunting odds. This story shows you that you can win, even when it looks like you should be defeated. It shows you can succeed even when your dreams are challenged.

This story begins in Dublin, Texas. As an Irishman, any story that starts in a town called Dublin has to be a good one. The young man that we're calling Benny, at the age of nine, watched his father pull the trigger of a gun and commit suicide.

Understandably, this tragedy would haunt Benny, distracting him for the rest of his life. After his father's suicide, Benny's family was very much in need of financial help. His mother, now on her own, couldn't reliably put the food on the table. Money was tight.

To help, Benny started selling newspapers. When he turned 11, he decided to become a caddie at a local country club. Local, in this case, meaning a six-mile trip. To be sure he wasn't tired by the time he arrived at the country club in the morning and to be sure he was first in line amongst the caddies, Benny sometimes slept in the bunkers—the sand traps. I can't imagine that was the best bed possible, but many nights it was Benny's bed.

He worked as a caddie at the country club throughout his adolescence, deciding, when he turned 17, that it was time to become a professional golfer. He competed on a professional tour for two years, which sounds exciting enough, but Benny wasn't really ready to go pro. The bottom line? Benny *failed*.

After two years on the road pursuing his dream, he came home a broken man. Desperate for money, he took whatever jobs he could get. Benny mopped floors, worked in gambling houses, worked as a local professional golfer, and crafted custom golf clubs. He took on whatever came his way that would help him earn and save money.

After several months, he decided to tour again. Unfortunately, the second time did not go any smoother than the first time, and he again returned home broke. He *failed* once again.

Now, the golf tour back in those days paid out very little prize money. Only golfers that finished in the top six (or maybe top ten) received any money. Sponsors were almost nonexistent. The winnings were often nothing more than pocket money, and pocket money was not what Benny was chasing. Only a tournament victory would count as success in Benny's eyes.

Twice Benny went on the road and shared rooms, travel expenses, and ate a ton of whatever the equivalent to Ramen noodles was way back then. He twice had to return home embarrassed by his failure. Twice he tried hard but did not succeed. He felt that he was "stuck" back home while his close friends were winning tournaments—and he wasn't. He was full of self-doubt. He was depressed. He admitted temporary defeat.

Back home for the second time, he knew he needed to regroup and try again. He continued to be haunted daily by the desire to win a tournament against the best golfers in the country. He felt a driving need to prove to himself he was that good. He also felt the need to prove to any of his doubters that he could do this.

Once again, he took on a bunch of jobs to save some more money, and, in the process, found the girl of his dreams and got married. He wanted to return to the golf tour, but also knew his head just wasn't right. However, his new wife knew what haunted him. She knew this obsession would not go away.

One day, the urge to compete became too strong for him to deny it any longer. Benny decided to go on the road one last time. He gave himself one last shot to follow his dream.

At first, things weren't very different. Then success started to find Benny, but at a cost. At the Texas Open in 1940, Benny finished the tournament tied for the lead with his close friend and childhood buddy, Byron Nelson. A playoff was held to determine the winner. Benny, best known to the golfing world as Ben Hogan, stuck his foot in his mouth during an interview before the big playoff. When asked what it felt like to be in a playoff with his good friend, Ben said, "Byron's got a good game, but it'd be a lot better if he'd practice. He's too lazy to practice." Everyone knew Ben as a very serious person and took his comment that way. Ben claimed that this comment was sarcastic in nature, meant as a joke, a little trash talk before the playoff, made in good-natured fun. Unfortunately, this explanation was never accepted by the public or Byron Nelson. Ben agonized over this slip up because he knew his frustration, obsession, and self-doubt were behind that comment, and that comment cost him a close friend. The relationship between the two golfers was never again what it once was. To make things worse, Ben lost in the playoff.

The good news is a few months later, after years of attempts, Ben Hogan won his first tournament.

His dream, his quest, his holy grail had been accomplished. The elusive victory was found, nine years after the chase for the dream began. Suddenly, Ben was relieved from all self-doubt. After the tournament win he is quoted as saying, "I was beginning to think I was an also-ran. I needed that win." In his mind, soul, and heart he had always wanted to succeed, and now he felt he had arrived.

After all of that, things snowballed. Ben had met the "Big Mo"—momentum. Anyone who follows golf knows that he became pretty darn successful. Over the following nine years, he went on to win 45 tournaments. Perhaps you are wondering, "What happened? Here's somebody who struggled and failed for years and suddenly wins another 45 tournaments the next nine years. How did he do it?"

What happened? Ben learned that he could actually win. That one win was enough to give him a lifetime of confidence.

Golfing experts say he worked harder than any golfer in history, that he practiced more than anyone. He practiced until his hands were actually bleeding. He practiced into the night. He practiced after dark just so that his swing and the mechanics of his game could be so automatic that he would be prepared for any challenge. Call it persistence. Yeah, I think that's fair. Yet, this isn't the end of the story.

Many of you may already know what happened at the end of those nine years of success, but I'll tell it anyway because it's important for the lesson we all need to learn. One night, when Ben was driving to a tournament, a Greyhound bus crossed over the centerline of the highway and hit his car head on. In an effort to protect his wife, Ben dove across the passenger seat and placed his body over hers. His wife Valerie incurred very minor injuries, but Ben wasn't so lucky. He ended up with a fractured collarbone, a fractured pelvis, a broken ankle, broken ribs, and an injured left eye. The injuries were so severe that the doctors seriously wondered if he would ever walk again, let alone play golf for a living.

Ben recovered much quicker and better than the doctors originally anticipated. This was good news, and everyone was hopeful that Ben had once again overcome the odds. However, on the day he was scheduled to go home, Ben collapsed. At first the doctors did not know what was wrong with Ben, only that his condition was life threatening and he needed help—now! They soon discovered that Ben had severe blood clots in his lungs and his heart, which they believe were caused by the accident.

A surgeon was flown in; emergency surgery was performed. The surgery was successful.

Another challenge for Ben. Dare we say another failure? For sure, this was another setback. The accident certainly had affected his life. He was faced with the prospect that he might never walk again and might never again play the game he loved so much.

But Ben wasn't done. He had more to prove. Sixteen months after the accident, Ben was back on the golf course. He was in extreme pain and his legs were extremely weak, but he played through the challenges, daunting as they were. He didn't just play; he actually *won* the U.S. Open.

Over the following nine years Ben won 10 more tournaments. Not only did he win those tournaments, but he also went on to become maybe the greatest golfer of all time. If not the very best, definitely one of the greatest.

Through his perseverance, practice, and mindset, he won 64 tournaments over the course of his life. Nine of his wins were major tournaments. He was considered to have the best swing in golf. For many years, the golf clubs he designed, built, and manufactured were considered the best quality golf clubs you could buy. (I know; my dad had a set!)

Hogan was recognized for his excellent focus. He was also honored for his course management; he knew how to work a course to his advantage. He turned golf into a thinking man's game and not just a game of physical ability. Ben was instrumental in taking golf into the marketplace and building it into the multi-billion dollar business it now is, helping to grow the PGA, the Professional Golfers Association. This is the golf tour that fans attend or watch on TV.

Before I investigated Ben's life, I only knew of Ben Hogan's remarkable comeback from his car accident. Without giving it a lot of thought, I assumed he was a natural, possibly an overnight success. His story tells us different.

What's in the story of little Benny? What can we learn from him? One thing is, like Ben, we always have to have hope. What's hope? Hope is optimism. It's peace. It's a sense of direction. It's motivation. It's momentum.

But perhaps the most important lesson we can learn from Ben Hogan is the fact that persistence really does pay off. Ben certainly demonstrated a huge dose of that!

Persistence, as defined by Rich DeVos, is "stubbornness with a purpose." That's a quote that has stuck with me for a very long time. I think persistence goes way beyond that definition, though. From my perspective, persistence is learning from our failures. It's an internal battle that's fueled by your higher power. (For me, that's God.) It involves doing whatever it takes to have victories. Persistence molds champions, and I believe it's your pathway to success.

Persistence is often blocked by the fear of failure. This fear could be a monetary fear—a fear of loss. It could be the fear of embarrassment—opinions of what other people think about you as you try to succeed. Sometimes social pressure can block you from action. Self-doubt, as we saw with Ben, can cause you massive confusion and pain.

To succeed, you must have faith in yourself and in your actions. Remind yourself that failure is only temporary and never final. Failure is a normal process and almost always one of the most essential building blocks of victories, dreams, and success.

Hope must also be coupled with persistence whenever you experience fear or are in a tough struggle. Look closely at whatever you face that feels like a failure or whatever isn't working in your life. Then, remember the persistence that Ben showed us as he practiced each day with passion and drive.

It's now your turn to practice persistence like Ben. Practice it with a boatload of hope, knowing that failure is part of a process, but trusting that your victories in life will amaze you. Practice having faith, not fear, each and every day. It's time to believe in the magic you have deep inside.

Follow your dreams! Success is ahead if you persist in hope.

ABOUT THE AUTHOR:

Doug Evans (**doug@discoveryourmissingpower.com**) is an accomplished executive coach, corporate trainer, author, CPA, and founder of several inspirational personal development sites on the Internet, including **www.discoveryourmissingpower.com**. Doug is an expert in masterminding with individuals or groups. His process can help you discover solutions to challenges you are facing and produce more money, more time, and more smiles, which will reignite your passion in daily living.

CHAPTER SEVENTEEN

The Cinderella Men
by Joel Johnson

"Never confuse a single defeat with a final defeat."

~F. Scott Fitzgerald

One of my favorite movies is the true story of the Great Depression era boxer, James J. Braddock, who in 1935 overcame great odds to win the world heavyweight boxing championship. By doing so, he took the title from Max Baer, despite the fact that he was the 10-1 underdog in the match.

James Braddock had great success in his first three years of boxing, reflected by his record of 44-2-2, including 21 knockouts. However, his boxing career declined after he lost a hard-fought match during which he fractured his right hand in several places.

His career went into a downward spiral after he fractured his hand a second time. It became harder and harder to get a boxing match. To make matters worse, the Great Depression hit, and jobs became very scarce. Just to put food on the table, he worked as a longshoreman anytime he got the chance, even though his hand had still not completely healed.

His life and career finally turned around in 1934 when he got a fight due to a late cancellation by another boxer. After winning it, he was set up to fight Max Baer for the world heavyweight boxing title. During that match, a reporter dubbed him "The Cinderella Man" because of his historical comeback from previous losses. Braddock won that match and held the world heavyweight title for two years.

I was inspired to title this chapter "The Cinderella Men" because I believe there are other men who, like James Braddock, have earned the name because of their great comebacks from previous losses. Below is the story of one such man.

I first heard the story of Andrew Duda in the mid-1970s from an uncle of mine who heard the story himself at one of A. Duda & Sons farms where he was testing some farm equipment that he had invented.

Andrew Duda was born in 1873 into a poor family in the small village of Velcice, which at that time was part of the Austro-Hungarian Empire (current day, Slovakia). Although it is not known what type of occupation he was in, it was likely farming, since that was the predominant occupation there.

For over a thousand years, his hometown of Velcice was mostly populated with Slovaks, who were an ethnic minority. That, coupled with the fact that he was a Lutheran in a largely Slovak Roman Catholic population, made him a religious minority within an ethnic minority. The disadvantageous condition of being in such a minority probably added to his motivation to immigrate to America.

Between 1899 and 1914, nearly 500,000 Slovaks, approximately 25 percent of the Slovaks living in the Austro-Hungarian Empire in 1910 immigrated to America. Both push and pull factors were at play, driving that record-setting immigration rate.

Overpopulation in the rural areas provided the "push" since the overabundance of people looking for farm work meant there was a surplus of workers and a scarcity of jobs. Those that were lucky enough to have a job received low wages and endured harsh working conditions. Many of them worked from sunrise to sunset, doing backbreaking work for less than 25 cents a day.

The "pull" was created by the American industrial revolution. Factory owners in the U.S. were so desperate for cheap labor that they often used recruiting agents to attract immigrant workers, sometimes even helping them with transportation costs. Another "pull" came from friends and relatives that had already immigrated and would write home with tales that made America seem like the "land of milk and honey" in comparison to their homeland. Some would write that they were now earning as much in a week as they had earned in a month back at home. (Often times they did not mention the hardships they faced in America or the numerous factory accidents that caused much loss of life and limb.)

Many of the Slovak immigrants chose Cleveland as their new home because factory jobs were plentiful there. By 1920, Cleveland had the largest population of Slovak immigrants in the United States.

The Slovak immigrants congregated together (as other ethnic minorities did) and mostly only associated with other Slovaks, since many native-born Americans did not agree with their religious and cultural beliefs. Andrew was fortunate to be able to stay with his wife's sister and her husband until he found a job and an apartment of his own.

Even some of the more established ethnic minorities showed disdain towards the Slovak immigrants and ridiculed their "old world" beliefs and dress. They resented the fact that the Slovaks were competing for the same unskilled labor jobs as they. Those prejudices towards the Slovaks may well have been one of the reasons Andrew Duda was eager to move away from the city to a rural area, such as what he was accustomed to in his homeland.

During his time in Cleveland, Andrew Duda was a member of the Holy Trinity Slovak Lutheran Church. When the pastor of the church heard that Andrew and some of the other parishioners were discontent with life in Cleveland and wanted to move to a rural area where they could raise their children "away from the evils of the big city," he suggested they call a meeting to discuss the situation.

Some at the meeting suggested Florida as a possible location because they had heard cheap land was available there due to a severe freeze in late 1894 and early 1895 that had killed most of the orange trees and wiped out the citrus industry. Although some orange tree grove owners replanted their groves, many could not afford to, so a lot of land that had been farmed was vacant.

Those at the meeting decided they wanted to learn more about the opportunity in Florida, so they asked the pastor and a fellow parishioner to go to Florida and investigate some potential locations. A few months later (in August 1911), another meeting was held and the two reported that they had identified three possible locations, all in Central Florida. Some members at that meeting were interested in the opportunity and formed the Slavia Colony Company for the purpose of purchasing land.

At least two more scouting parties were sent out before the group finally decided on a site for their colony. In October of 1911, the Slavia Colony Company purchased 1200 acres of land about 15 miles northeast of Orlando for $17,400.

Andrew contracted to purchase ten of the 1200 acres. He and some of the others who also purchased parcels left Cleveland soon afterwards (in February of 1912) to start their new lives in Florida.

Most of the soon-to-be property owners had envisioned their "new home" to be their "holy land," so you can probably imagine their surprise when they stepped off of the train and saw their new accommodations—wooden shacks that had previously housed African-American turpentine workers.

The shacks had spaces between the boards that were almost as large as the boards themselves. It was February, so they soon found out that their new "houses" provided little protection from the cold. A few months later, when the weather turned warm, they learned that they also afforded little if any protection from the swarms of mosquitos. For a time, Andrew stayed with another family since there weren't enough shacks for all of the settlers. After his family arrived, they were able to have their own shack, which they also shared with others who needed housing.

Although there was an artesian well on the property, the water it provided had a strong sulfuric taste. It would be a long while before they could afford to have a deep well dug that would give them better tasting water.

The housing conditions were dismal and the condition of the property was just as bad—much of the property was low-lying muck land that would have to be drained before it could be farmed. Most of it was covered with palmettos, cypress trees, and pine trees (not to mention a fair number of alligators) that would have to be removed through backbreaking labor. It was far from an auspicious start for Andrew. He likely could not envision the agricultural empire that A. Duda & Sons would someday be.

A few months after Andrew arrived in Slavia, his wife and children left their hometown of Velcice and started the long trip to America. They arrived in the U.S. at New York City and processed thru the Ellis Island Immigration Station before traveling on to Florida. Finding the train that would take them to Florida was difficult since Katarina didn't speak English. However, she finally met a Polish couple that she was able to communicate with that helped her find the correct train. There apparently was not much communication between Andrew and Katarina before she and the children left Velcice because when they arrived in Slavia, Andrew was so surprised to see them that he was speechless. Later he said that [upon seeing them] he thought he had died and gone to heaven.

A kitchen garden provided them with plenty of vegetables, but they were lucky if they had meat on their plates more than once a week. There were many things they needed that required cash, which was in very short supply. When they had more vegetables than they could eat, they would take the excess to the farmers market in Orlando to earn money. As they gradually cleared more of their ten acres, they were able to sell more of the crops at the market.

When Andrew wasn't working to clear his ten-acre plot, he did whatever work he could find to raise cash. He labored for timber companies, pulling cypress stumps out of the swamps with oxen, worked at a nearby packing plant, collected turpentine from the pine trees, and performed any other work he could find. He even talked the county into paying him to transport the children of Slavia to school a few miles away with a horse-drawn covered wagon.

Joseph Duda (Andrew Duda's grandson, who retired as CEO of A. Duda & Sons in 2010) said in a 2010 newspaper article that his grandparents were "dirt-poor immigrants" and that his father and uncles often didn't have shoes to wear so the teachers at the school they attended would take up a collection for them.

Church records documented that the church council on more than one occasion made him loans from the church's building fund, and that he sometimes had trouble repaying the loans on time, even though some of them were for as little as twenty dollars. Duda helped establish the church and would later become one of its biggest benefactors. The church is still in existence and Andrew's family is still one of its biggest benefactors.

Despite all of his efforts, Andrew couldn't make a profit from the farm, so after exhausting all of his resources and struggling to make the mortgage payments, he returned to Cleveland to raise more capital. Four years after arriving in Slavia, the family packed up and headed back to the factories.

Katarina and their three sons joined Andrew working in the factories or on the truck farms in the area. Finally, after 10 years, they had saved enough money to return to Florida and start again.

When they returned to Slavia in 1926, Andrew planted a crop of celery, and this time his faith, perseverance, and hard work was rewarded with a profit. With that successful crop, A. Duda & Sons was born. Although there would be more obstacles, Andrew and his family would never again have to work in the factories.

Andrew Duda passed from this life in 1958 at age 84, but what he started has continued on and is flourishing under the direction of his descendants.

A. Duda & Sons has come a long way in the 90 years since they grew their first successful crop on that small 10-acre plot that Andrew Duda purchased from the Slavia Colony Company.

They are one of the largest farming operations in the U.S., with locations in Florida, Texas, California, and Arizona. In 2014, the company generated gross revenues of $441 million.

The company is still family-owned. There are about 100 owners, six of whom are on the board of directors (along with four outside directors). In addition to their agricultural operations, they created a master-planned community a few years ago, began a homebuilding operation, and, more recently, started a commercial real estate portfolio.

The focus of this story has been on Andrew Duda Sr., since he provided the initial faith, vision, and perseverance that laid the foundation of the A. Duda & Sons farming empire. However, I don't want to minimize the contributions of his wife, three sons, and the later generations of Dudas. Their efforts were certainly key in building the company to its current stature.

It is worth noting that all three of Andrew Duda's sons were inducted into the Florida Agricultural Hall of Fame in 1985. It is further worth noting that three of his grandsons were also inducted into the same hall of fame in 2015.

Andrew Duda succeeded in what many would consider to be the three most important areas of life—faith, family, and finances. He did it by having a dream that he was willing to work hard for and never quitting until he achieved it.

ABOUT THE AUTHOR

Joel Johnson got "hooked" on personal development books at the young age of 21 after being encouraged by his older brother, Vic, to start reading them. He used the principles learned from reading books such as *How To Win Friends And Influence People*, by Dale Carnegie, *The Greatest Salesman In The World*, by Og Mandino and others, to co-found two different businesses by the time he was 25.

Joel started developing his writing skills while president of a non-profit organization, which published his articles in their monthly newsletter. He currently writes articles for his own personal development website, SelfTalk4Success.com, which is dedicated to helping others develop their self-talk skills.

When it's time to "kick-back" he enjoys "fishing from his dock," gardening with his wife, Lisa or by just relaxing, "doing nothing in particular."

He can be reached by email at **joel@SelfTalk4Success.com**

CHAPTER EIGHTEEN

What to Do Now
by Vic Johnson

"There are no mistakes in life, there are only lessons."

~ Mark Twain

Let's end with a question: When does failure happen?

Does it happen when an obstacle gets in your way? Over the course of this book, you've seen many obstacles either dismissed or overcome on the path to success. So it's hard to say that an obstacle is the defining moment of failure.

Does it happen when you change your career path, or your strategy? No, in fact many people find their greatest successes in life when they do exactly that. They take lessons from obstacles and "failures" and use them to strengthen themselves, not to beat themselves up over it.

Does failure happen when you have no more money? That's obviously not the case, as there are countless examples of people who have risen to wealth and success from very little.

Does failure happen when you take a break? No, sometimes success happens even after you take a break and come back to your goals even stronger.

So when does failure happen?

If you're sensing the pattern here, you understand that failure only happens when *you* decide it happens. Only you have the power to stop yourself from trying. Only you have the decision to make. You're the single decider of what is a success and what is a failure, and that fact will never change…

…unless your thoughts change.

The way you perceive success and failure will have a greater impact on your actions than you can ever know. There are too many of us who let our failures get under our skin. If you've ever encouraged a friend who wanted to give up after only one try, you know what this perspective means. Yet when failure happens to *us*, we change our tune. We want to give a single failure all of the emotional relevance we can because it's so hard to deal with.

But once you realize that failure is a matter of perspective, you'll start to see more and more opportunities in your life. You'll start to see the good that can evolve from rejections. You'll start to see the value of an editor suggesting revisions to your story, or the potentiality that the reason you were declined for a job wasn't that you're a failure, but because the job really wasn't right for you after all.

There are many failures that have either been successes in disguise or have helped people learn the path to success. Failure is something of a guidance system that lets you know how close you really are to the best path. If you don't listen to failure, you might go all over the map. But if you listen *too much* to failure, you might make the opposite mistake: you might stop before you even give yourself a real chance.

Now that you understand this, let's take a look at some of the best ways to form a new perspective on failure in your own life.

Five Superior Interpretations for Failures

Get out a piece of paper and write down one of your recent failures. Then, come back to this text and write down the following questions:

- Is there some silver lining in this failure that can actually help me move forward?

- Is this failure really as devastating as it seems, or am I just making a mountain out of a molehill?

- Can I continue going after my dream? Am I physically able to do so?

- Is there some feedback I can learn from this failure that will strengthen my motivation to continue in the future?

- Is this failure final?

You'll find that after answering these questions, your perspective completely changes. Obviously, the answer to the question, "Is this failure final?" tends to be *no*, of course it's not final. But as you search yourself for answers to the other four questions, you'll find yourself coming up with legitimate reasons why the failure might have been *good* for you in the long run.

It might seem counterintuitive, but many people don't actually know what is best for them. It's only *after* the fact that they realized they were seeking after the wrong thing.

There are many examples of famous "failures" who found their success in an unexpected place. The cartoonist Scott Adams, creator of the *Dilbert* comic strip, has detailed his life in the business world and all of the successes and failures he's endured along the way. Somewhere along the line, the idea for a new cartoon popped into his head, and now he's one of the most recognizable cartoonists in the world.

This isn't to say that *your* path will be unexpected. You may indeed have few failures on the road to success in your original chosen field. But it's an important lesson: failure is not final, but it can teach us some valuable things about ourselves.

Action Steps to Get You Started

Now that we've explored the possibility that failure is indeed not final, it's time to put this new perspective into action. It's time to look at the world from this new vantage point and take the steps that will produce real and lasting change in your life.

1. **Begin by writing down your goal.** Try to be specific about what you want. Rather than saying, "I want to be a successful salesperson," you might say, "I earn 150,000 dollars in commissions by December 31, _____." This helps to make your action steps that much more concrete.

2. **Make a list of the failures you're willing to endure to reach your goal.** To stick with our salesperson example, you might have to develop thick skin and endure daily rejection when you make sales calls. Try to think of other potential failures as well, such as missing out on a sale at the last moment.

3. **Write down how those failures can be used constructively.** In the case of missing out on a sale at the last moment, you might write down how that's a specific event that can teach you not to lose those sales in the future. Try to find the constructive work that can be done after a failure, including what you'll need to learn from the failure.

4. **Give yourself a "failure number."** Tell yourself that you're simply going to give yourself a chance, and that after X

amounts of failures, you'll revisit your goals. This isn't a reason to quit; instead, it's a way to change the way you view a specific failure. It "reframes" the idea of failure and lessens the potentially negative impact of each individual hiccup.

5. **Ask yourself what you're willing to go through in order to achieve your goal.** One of the most powerful success tips of all time is determine what price you are willing to pay for your goal and then pay that price. If you know what you're getting into from the beginning, you'll constantly be reminded of how life changing your goal really is and what it means to you to earn it. Failures will "lose their luster" along the way because of your long-term perspective.

From there, create a list of milestones that you'll have to achieve on your way to your goal. Try to make them action steps rather than specific goals in and of themselves... you don't want to give yourself *too* many goals to manage! For example, if you want to publish a book, you might say "write 750 words per day" or "submit to three editors this week." It's that simple. At this point, you're not focused on the failures. You're focused on the action steps along the way.

Focusing on these action steps will enable you to feel like you've achieved a goal even though you have not yet reached your ultimate goal. If you constantly feel that you're at least doing what you know in your heart you *need* to be doing to eventually achieve success, you're going to tolerate failure much better than someone who doesn't have a systematic approach. When you focus more on your actions rather than the results of those actions, you don't give as much emotional relevance to each individual rejection and failure.

And that's really the goal.

After all, we all fail. Michael Jordan is the greatest basketball player of all time, yet he's missed many a game-ending shot. J.K. Rowling created one of the most beloved series ever, yet she wasn't born with wonderful stories already fully developed in her brain. It takes serious work and commitment to achieve success—and that means having dedication that goes *beyond* failure. It means having the belief that no failure is ever final so long as you're in charge of your own actions.

Nelson Mandela, once imprisoned for many years, clung to a poem called *Invictus.* He kept his dignity and his sanity because he knew that it wasn't circumstances that determined the success of the individual—it was his or her own response to those circumstances.

You have a similar power in your own life.

You have the strength to say, "This failure is not final."

Now, will you use it?

> Out of the night that covers me,
> Black as the pit from pole to pole,
> I thank whatever gods may be
> For my unconquerable soul.
>
> In the fell clutch of circumstance
> I have not winced nor cried aloud.
> Under the bludgeonings of chance
> My head is bloody, but unbowed.
>
> Beyond this place of wrath and tears
> Looms but the Horror of the shade,
> And yet the menace of the years
> Finds, and shall find me, unafraid.
>
> It matters not how strait the gate,
> How charged with punishments the scroll,
> I am the master of my fate:
> I am the captain of my soul.

ABOUT VIC JOHNSON

Vic Johnson was totally unknown in the personal development field fifteen years ago. Since that time he's created some of the most popular personal development sites on the Internet. One of them, AsAManthinketh.net, has given away over 400,000 copies of James Allen's classic book.

A seven-time Amazon best-selling author, he's become an internationally known expert in goal achieving and hosted his own TV show, Goals 2 Go, on TSTN. He has become a powerful authority in the self-publishing field and has taught thousands how to publish their first book. His three-day weekend seminar events, Claim Your Power Now, attracted such icons as Bob Proctor, Jim Rohn, Denis Waitley and many others.

This success has come despite the fact that he and his family were evicted from their home twenty years ago and the next year his last automobile was repossessed. His story of redemption and victory has inspired subscribers from around the world as he has taught the powerful principles that created incredible wealth in his life and many others.

For a free copy of his best-selling book *How To Write A Book This Weekend, Even If You Flunked English Like I Did* go to:

http://EbookMentor.com

Vic Johnson's websites include:

AsAManThinketh.net

Goals2Go.com

GettingRichWitheBooks.com

TheChampionsClub.org

MyDailyInsights.com

VicJohnson.com

ClaimYourPowerNow.com

BOOKS BY VIC JOHNSON

Day by Day with James Allen

How To Write A Book This Weekend, Even If You Flunked English Like I Did

Goal Setting: 13 Secrets of World Class Achievers

It's Never Too Late And You're Never Too Old: 50 People Who Found Success After 50

52 Mondays: The One Year Path To Outrageous Success & Lifelong Happiness

The Magic of Believing: Believe in Yourself and The Universe Is Forced to Believe In You

Self Help Books: The 101 Best Personal Development

How I Created a Six Figure Income Giving Away a Dead Guy's Book

50 Lessons I Learned From The World's #1 Goal Achiever

How To Make Extra Money: 100 Perfect Businesses for Part-Time and Retirement Income

You Become What Your Think About

www.ingramcontent.com/pod-product-compliance
Lightning Source LLC
LaVergne TN
LVHW051836080426
835512LV00018B/2905